ENRIQUE ZALDIVAR

Infinite
LINE

Pen and ink drawings

Imaginative works, landscapes, still lifes and wild life

Volume 1

Infinite Line (Volume 1)

Drawings, texts and graphic design:
Enrique Zaldivar

English revision:
Marc David Gambino
Alfredo Artesona

Copyright © 2019 Enrique Zaldivar

ISBN: 9781792800023

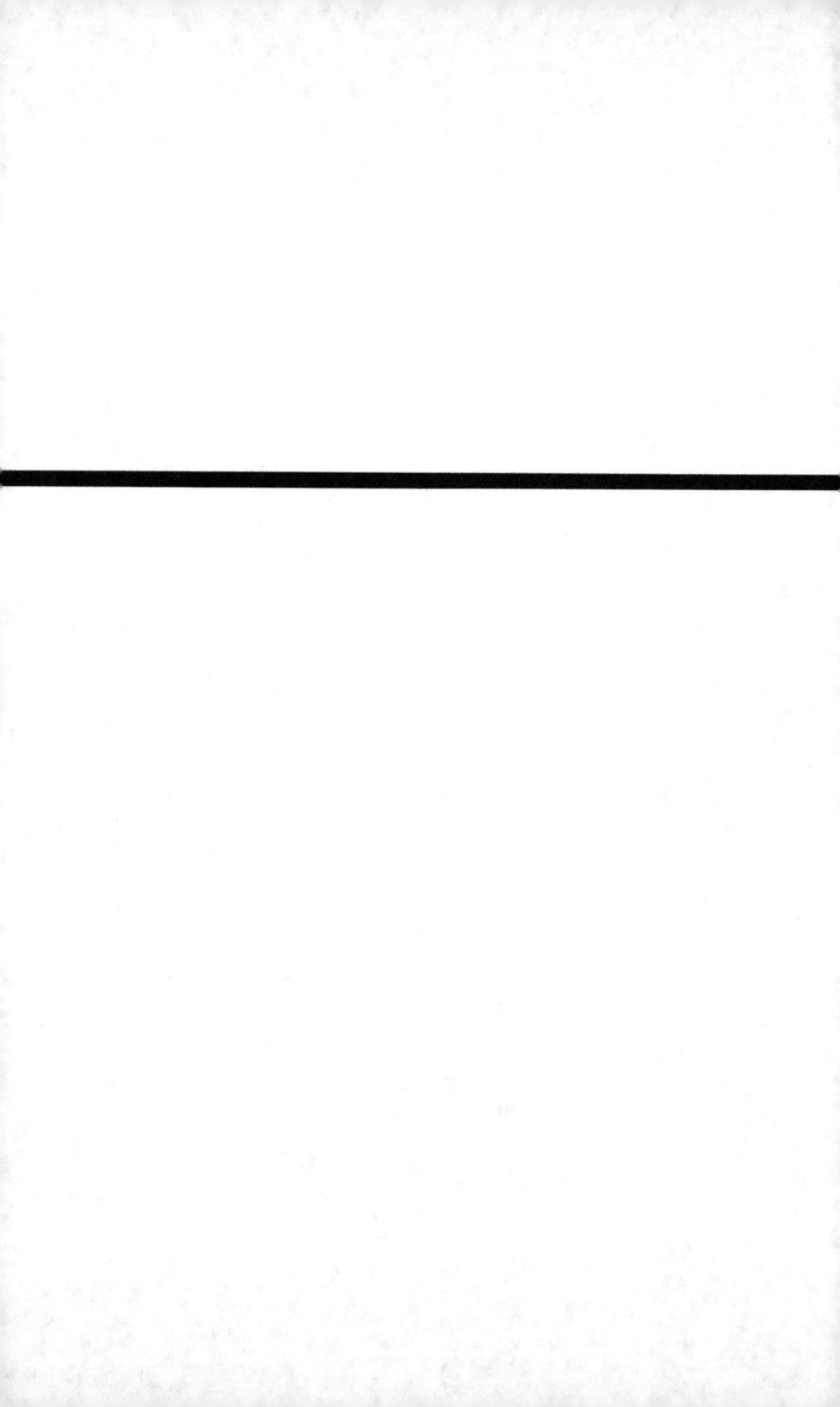

Delusions

Facing freedom

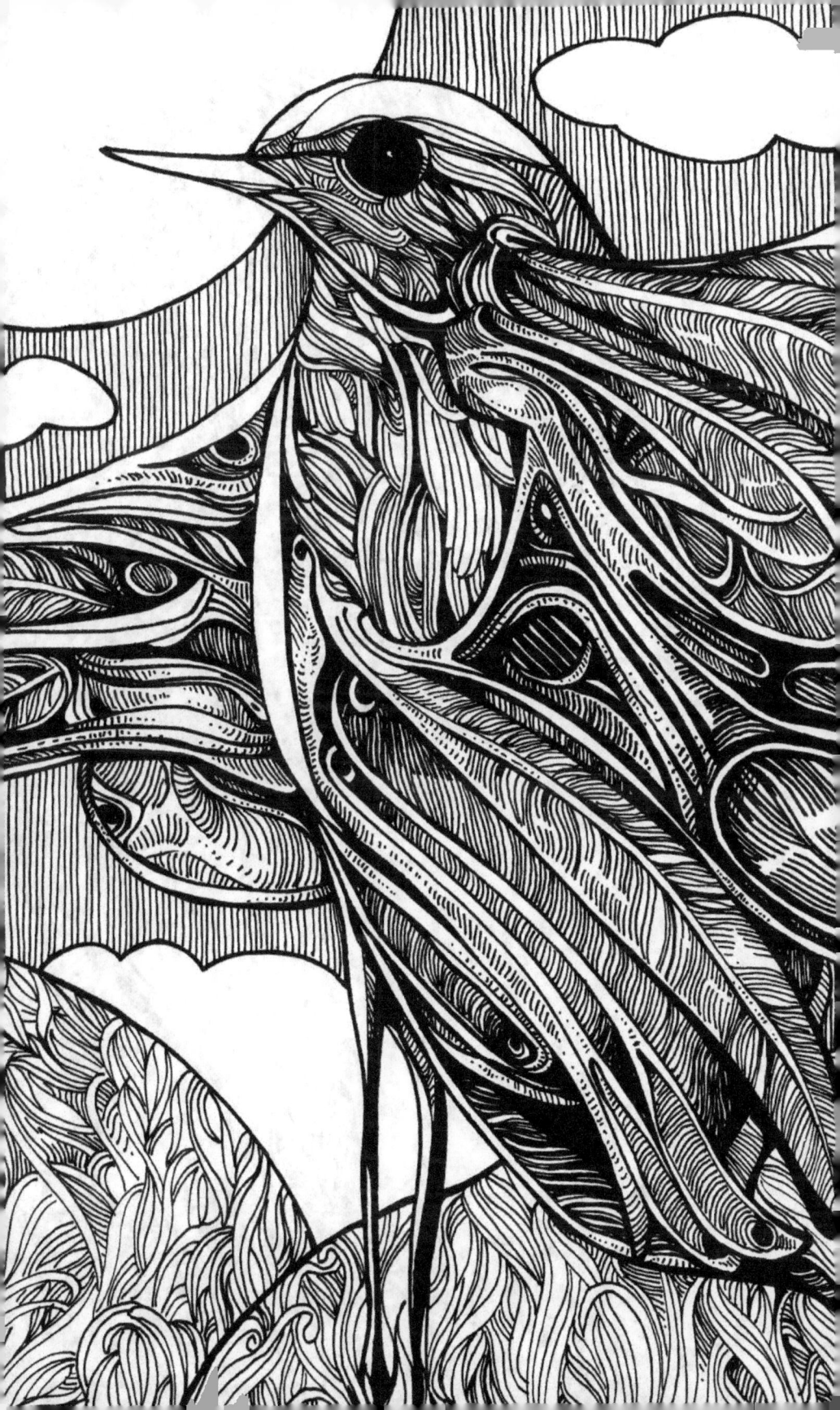

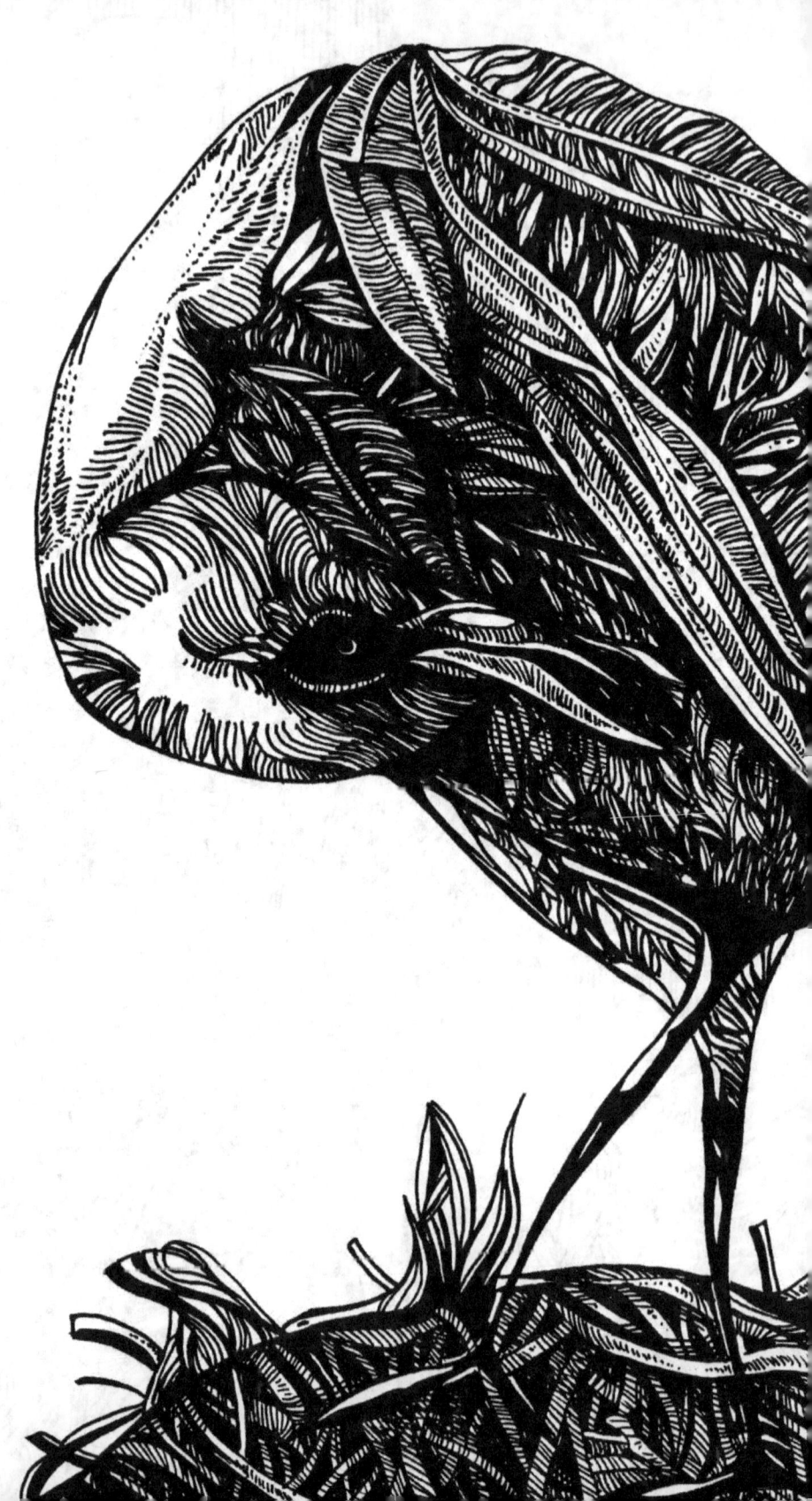

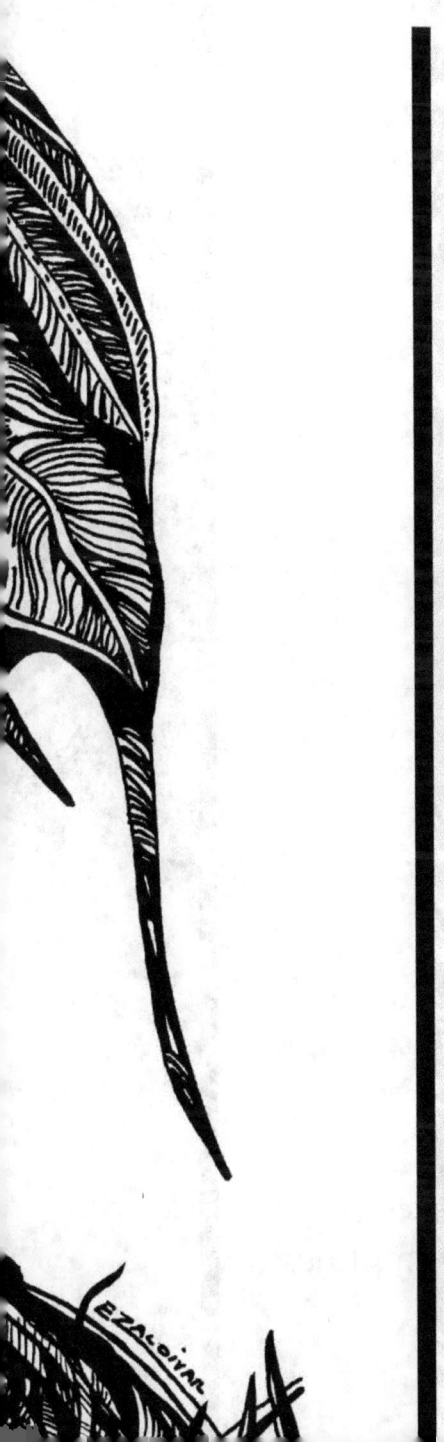

What do I want wings for?
Could I reach the limits of heaven?

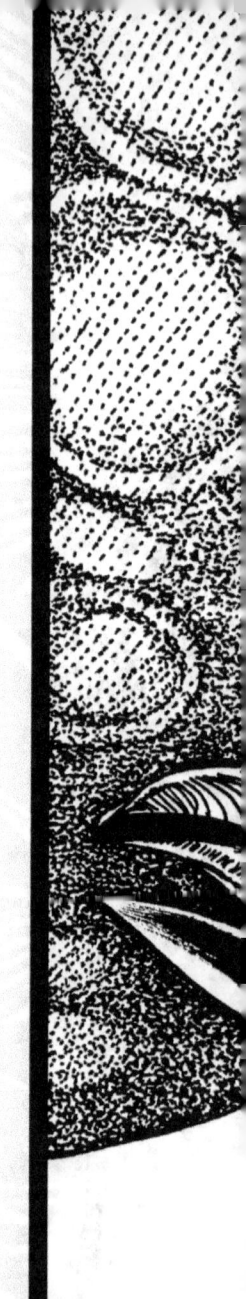

You can not save me from the free
fall and the infinite leap into emptiness

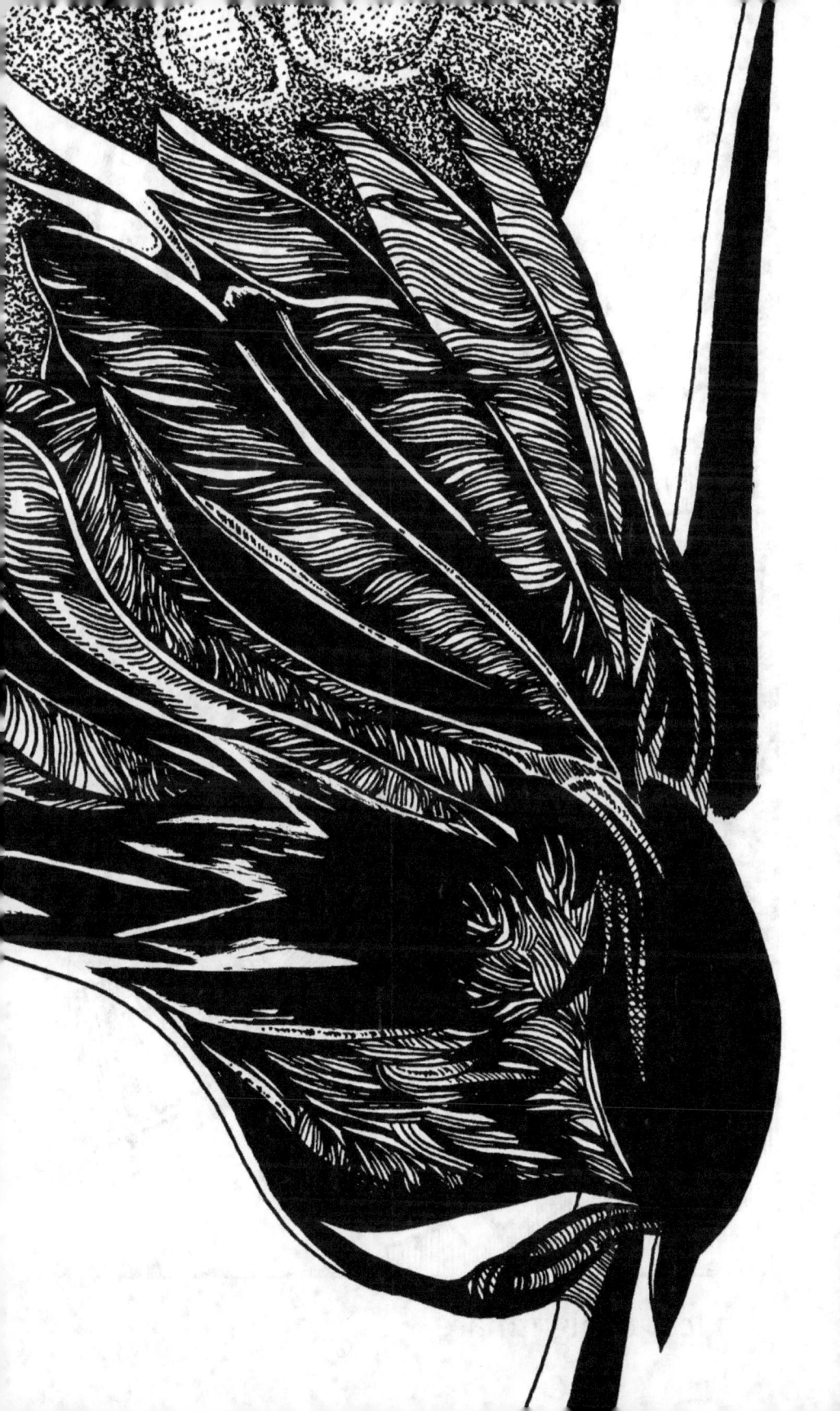

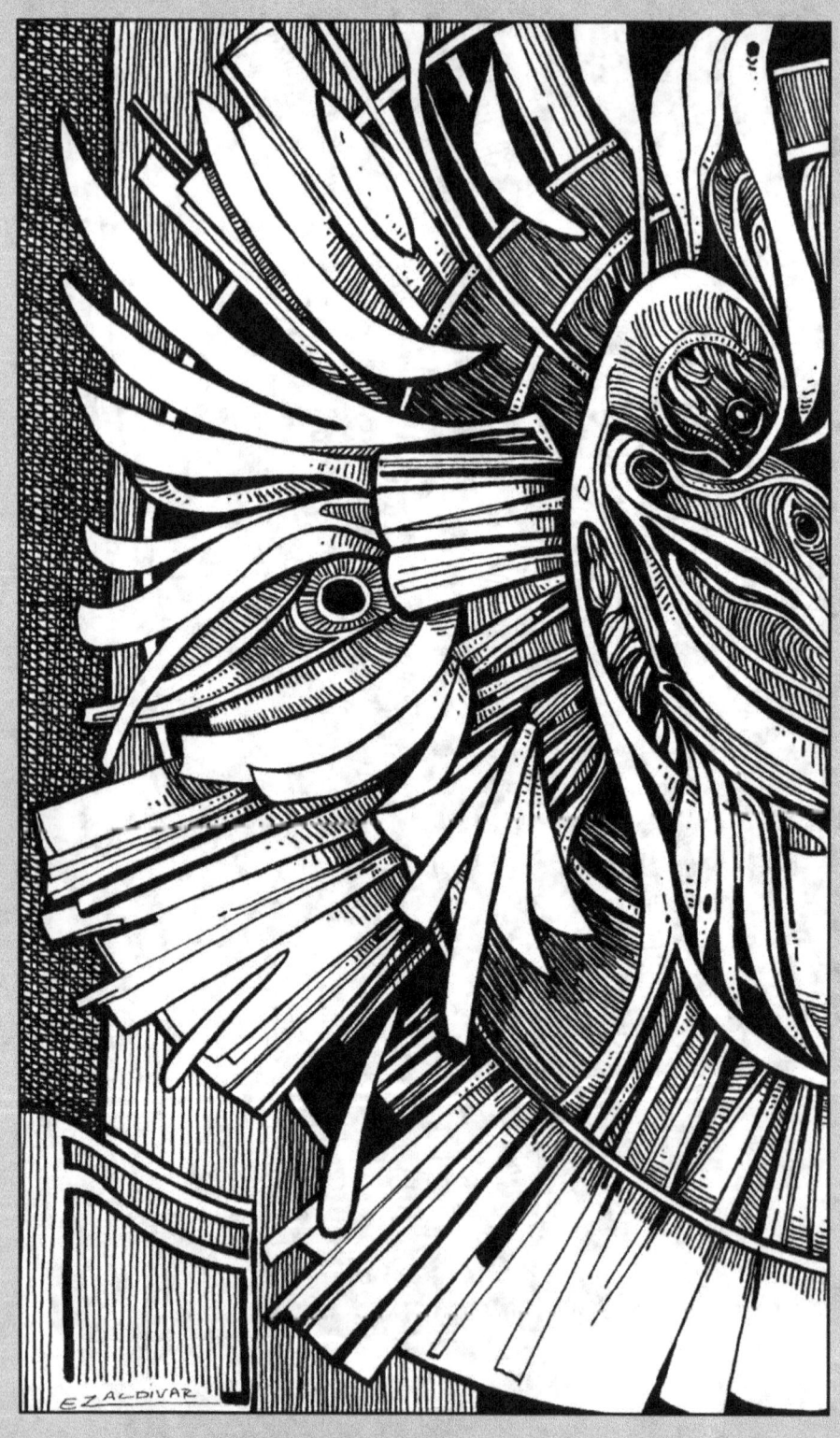

The Icarus nightmare

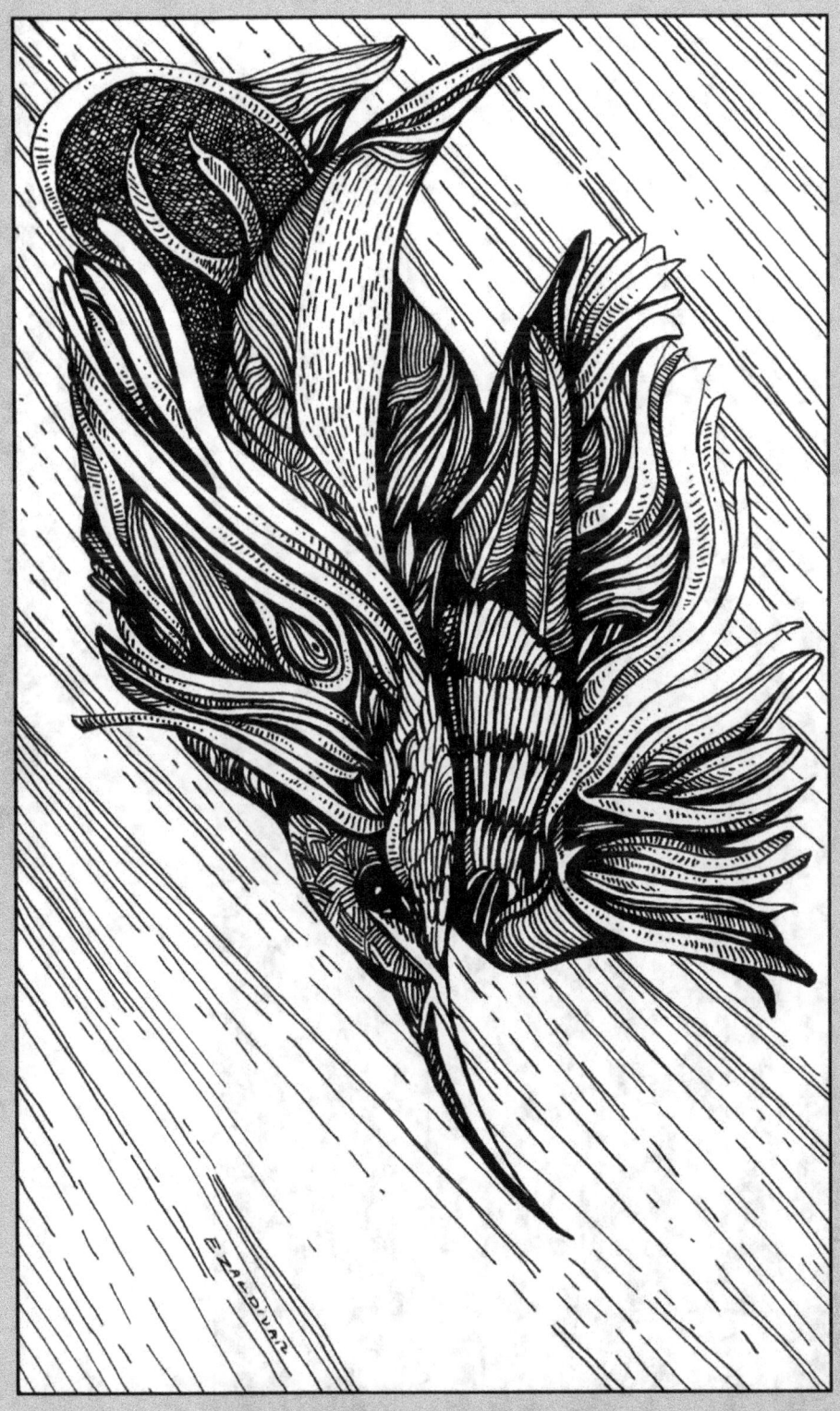

Vertigo

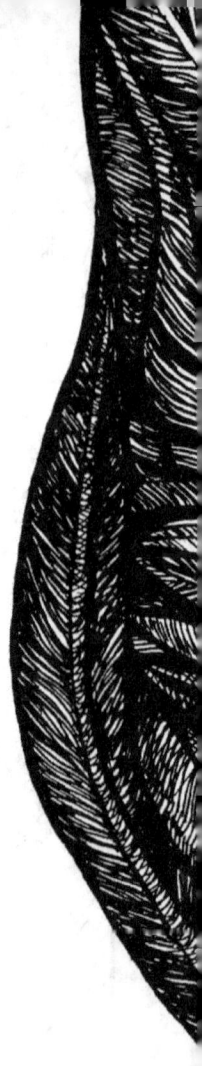

Tied to the nothing

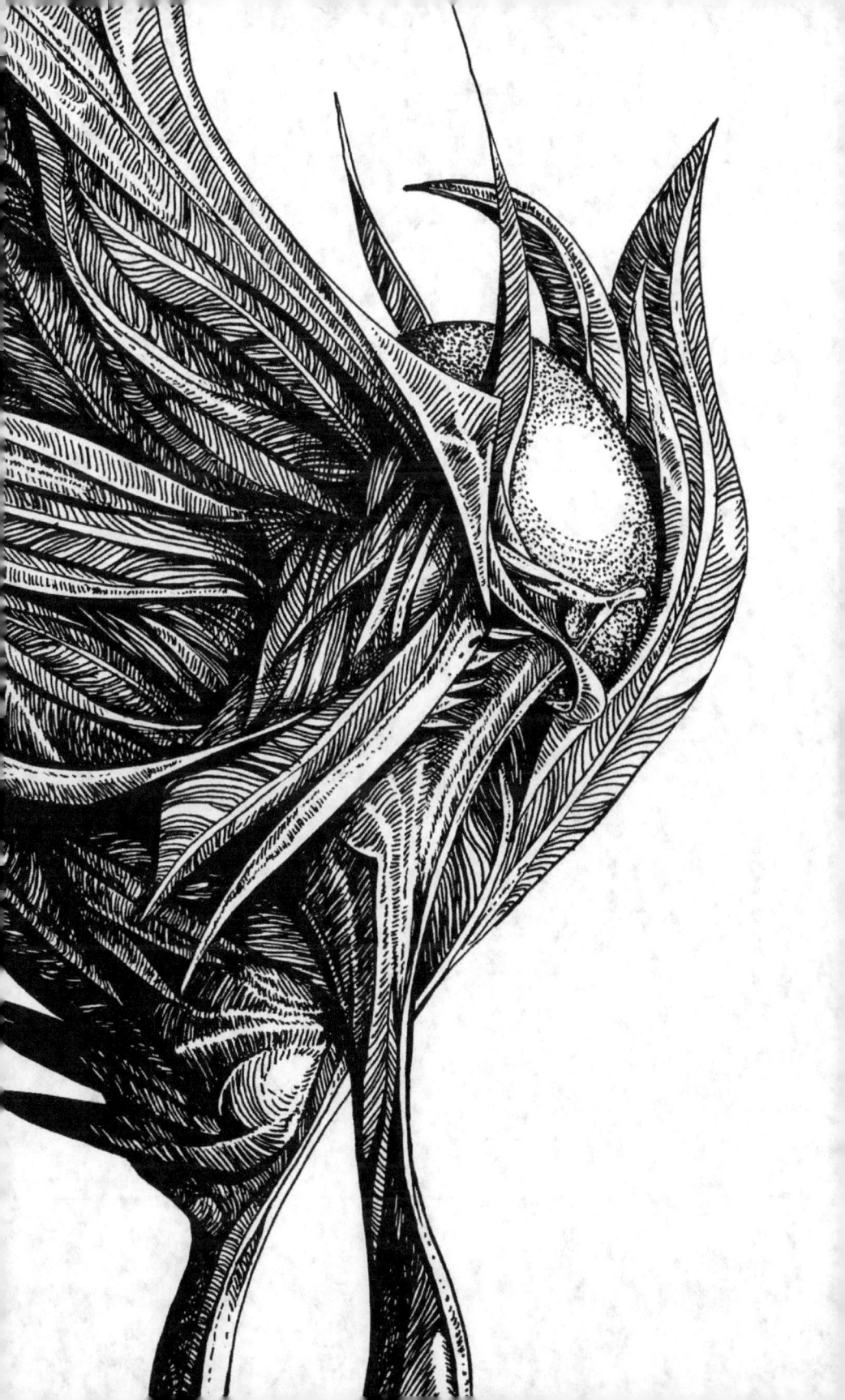

Voices to the wind

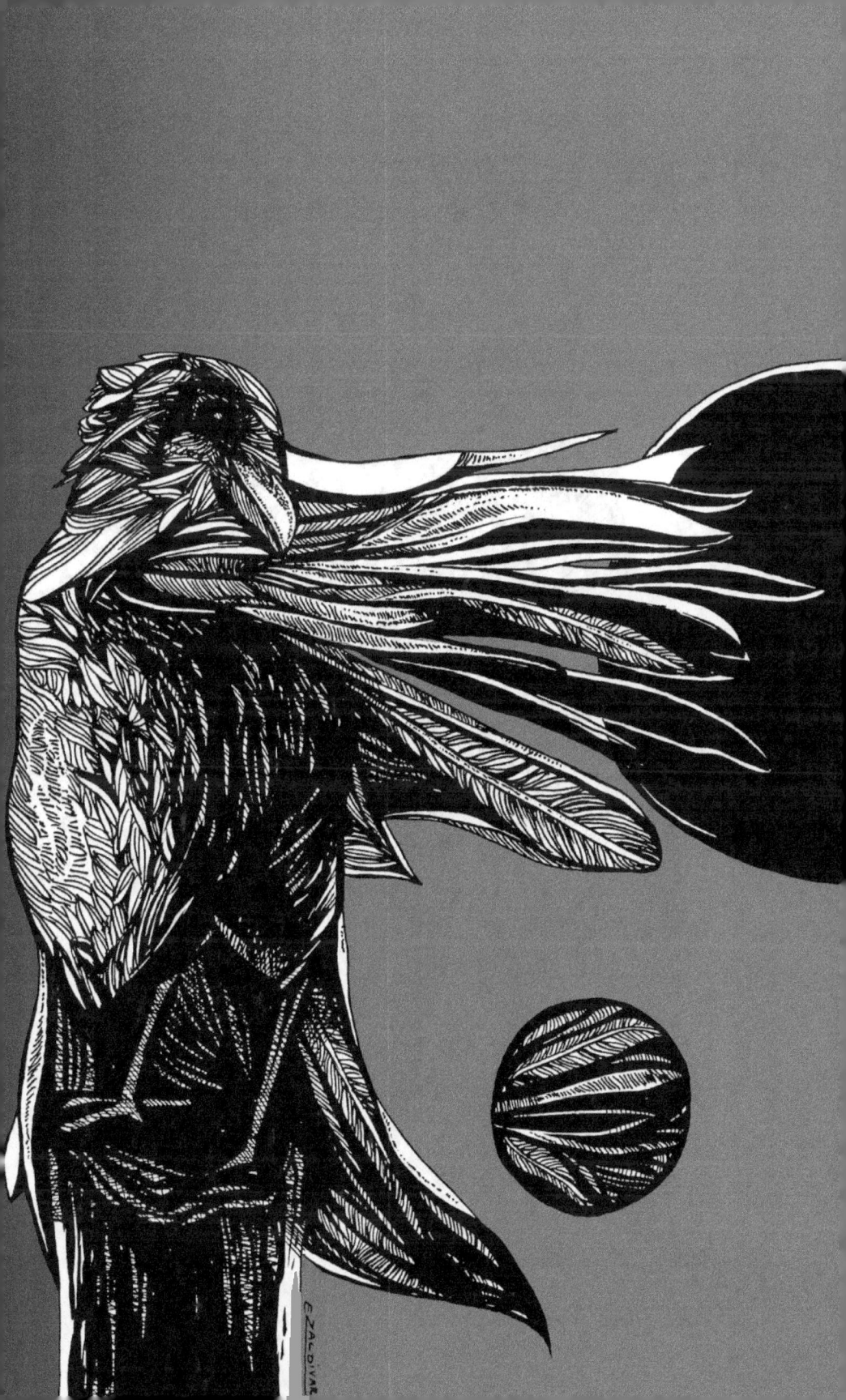

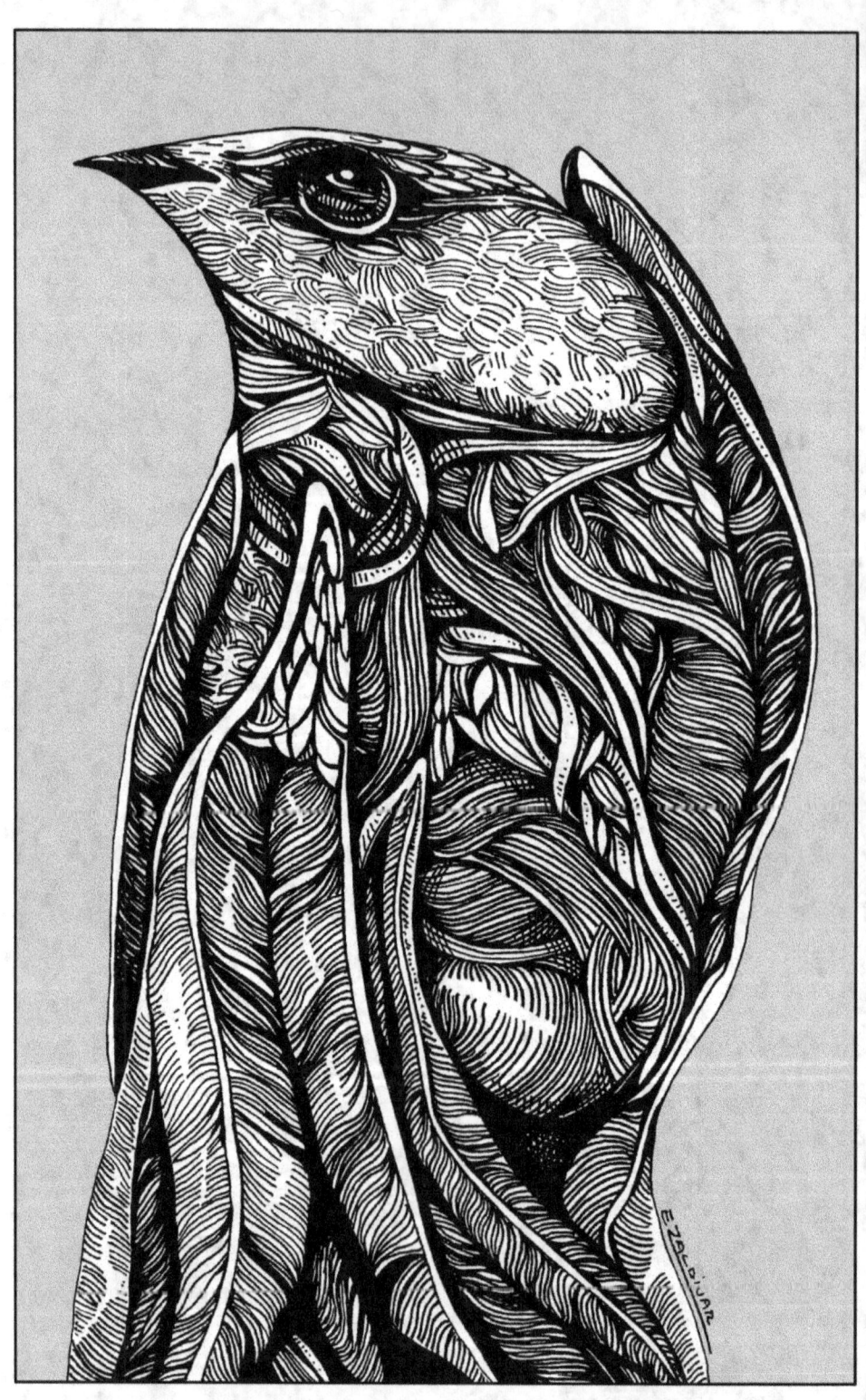

Contemplative

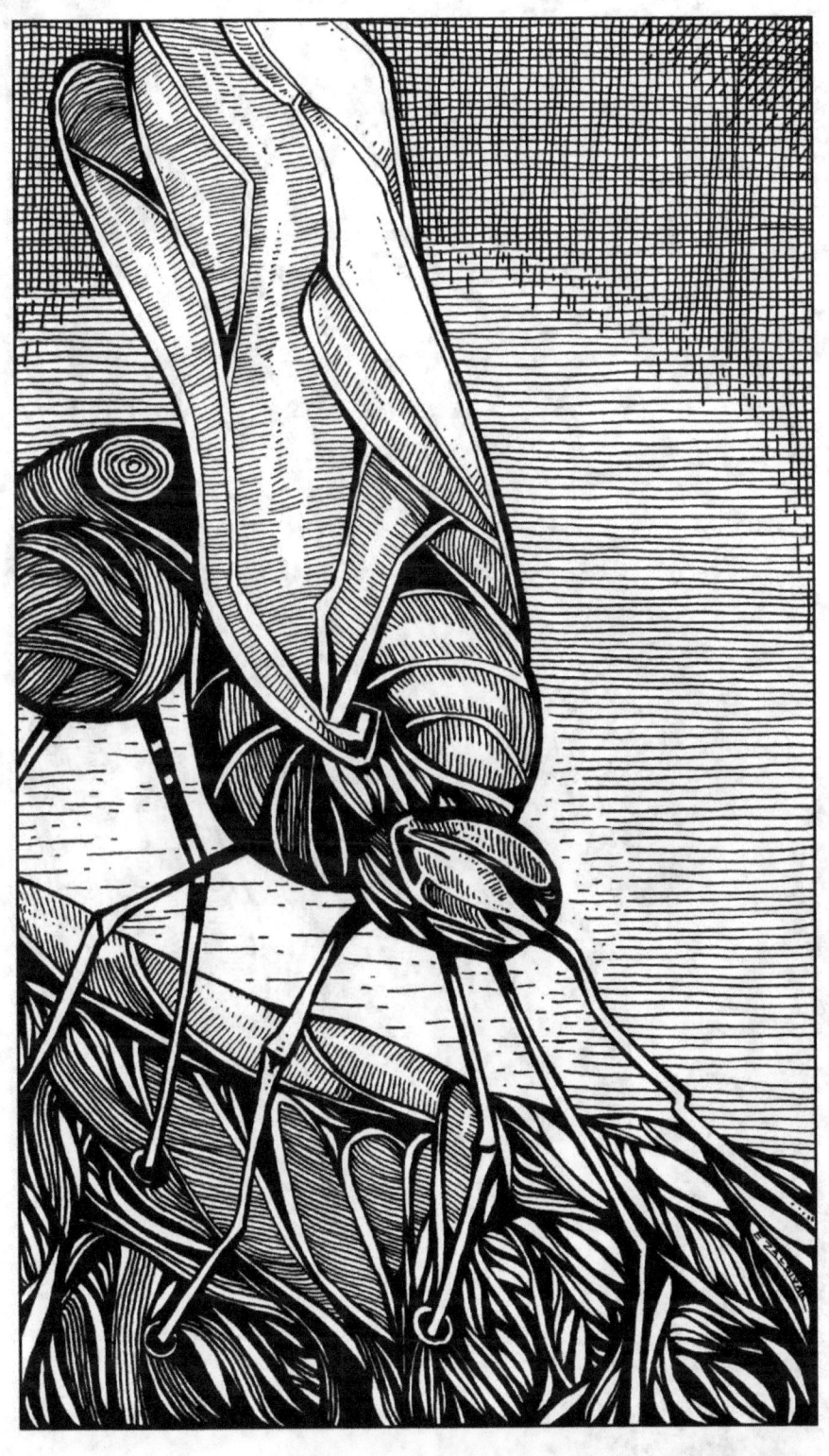

Insects, lights and labyrinths

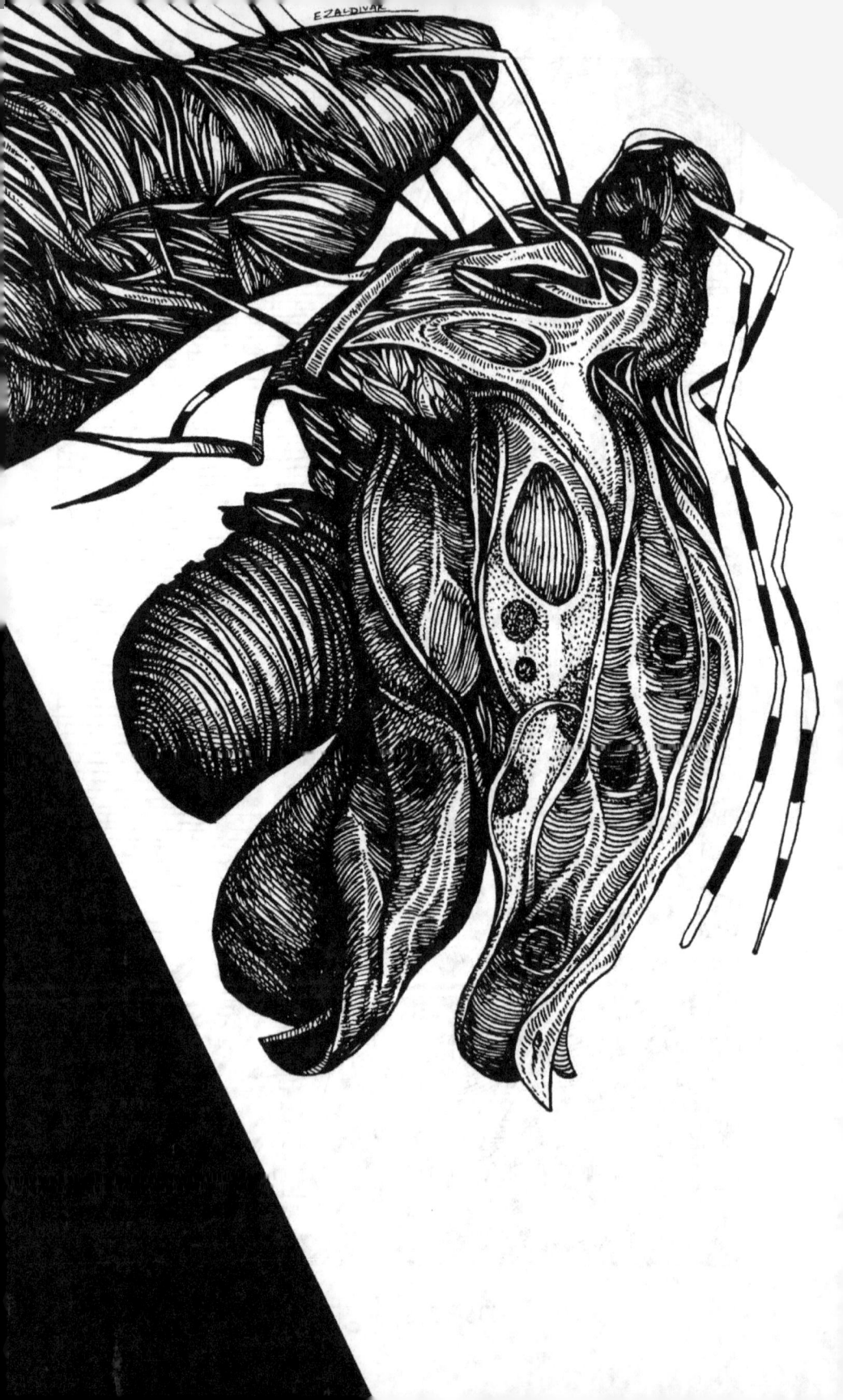

Infinite metamorphosis

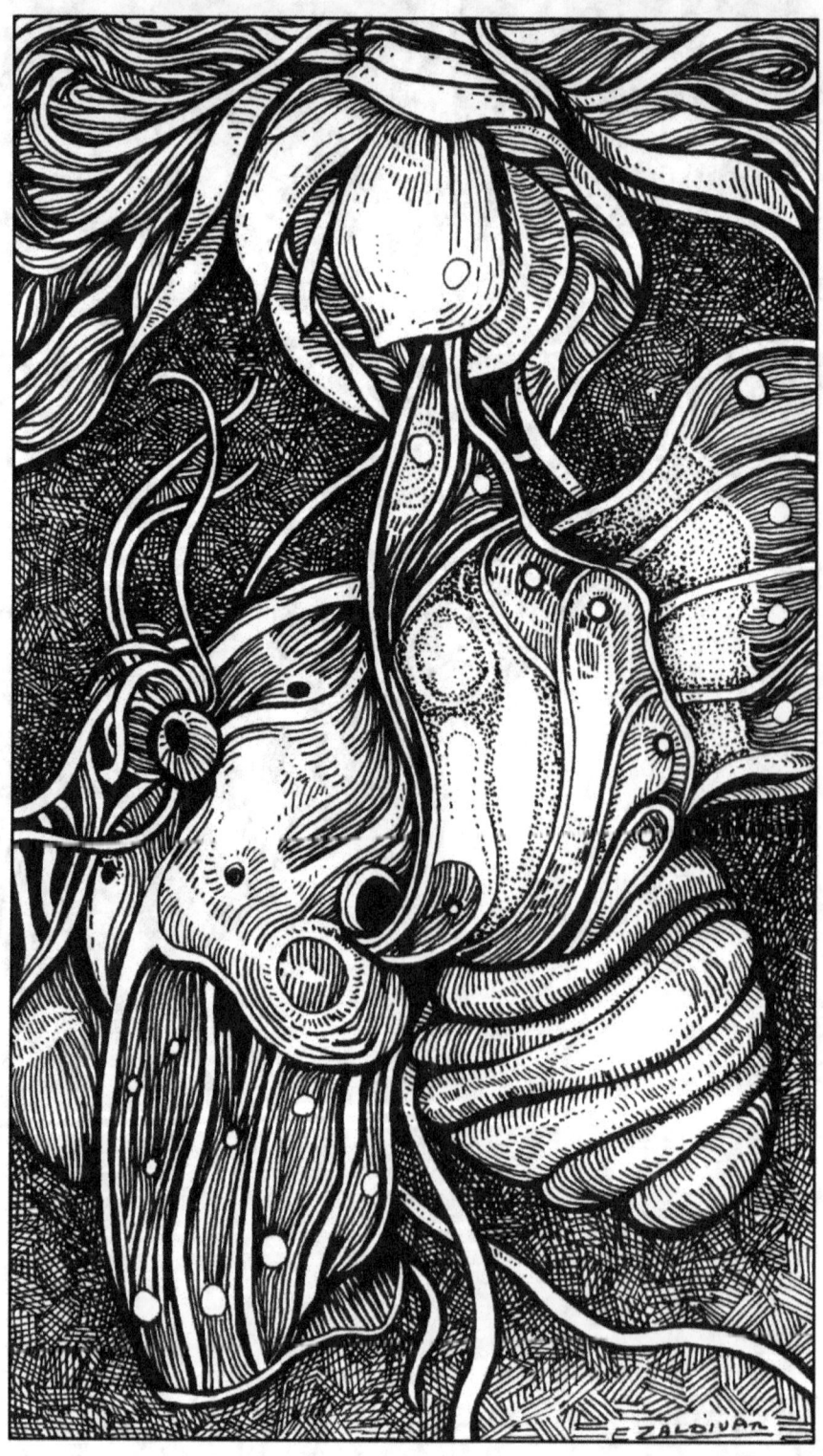

Chrysalis

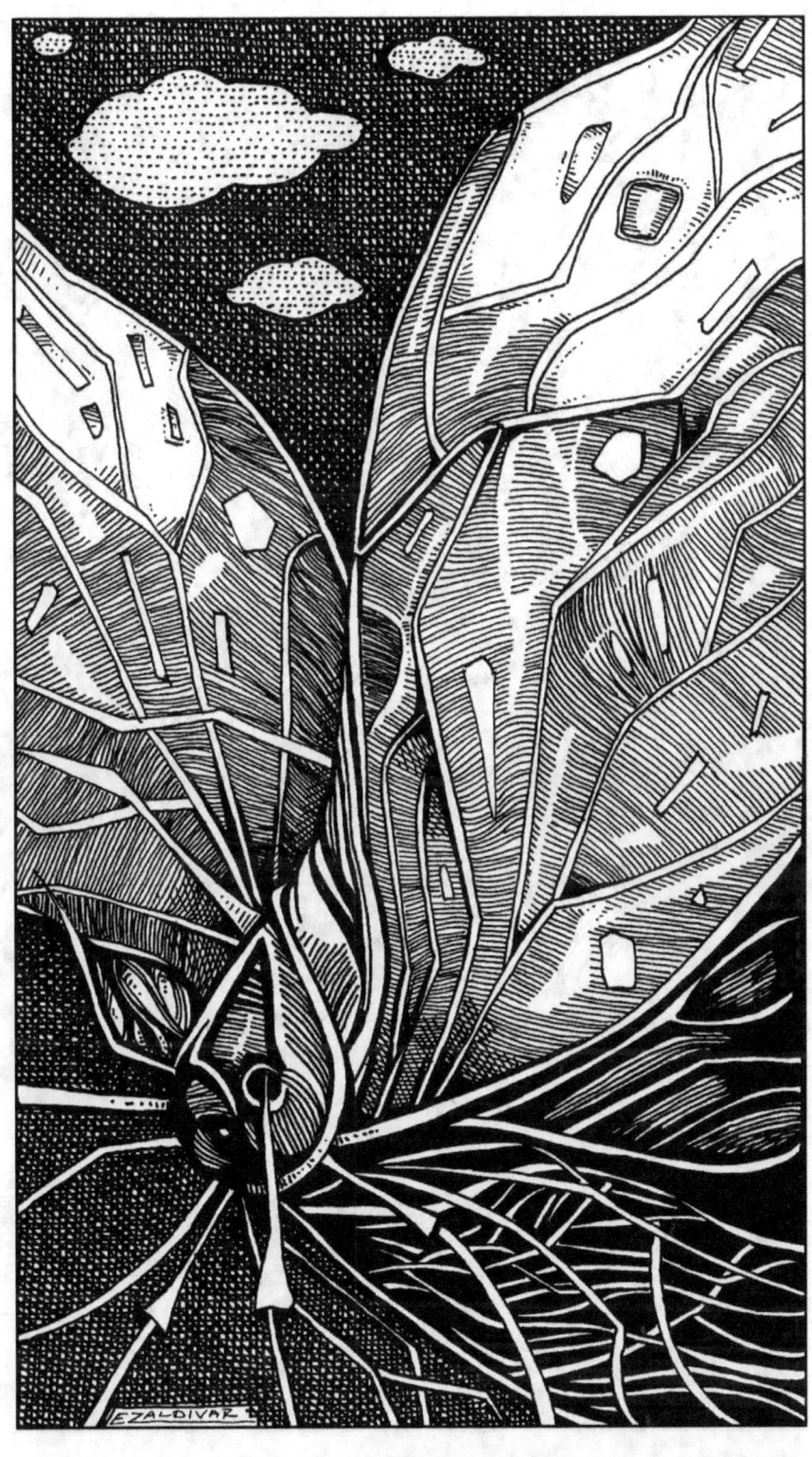

Flight of the butterflies

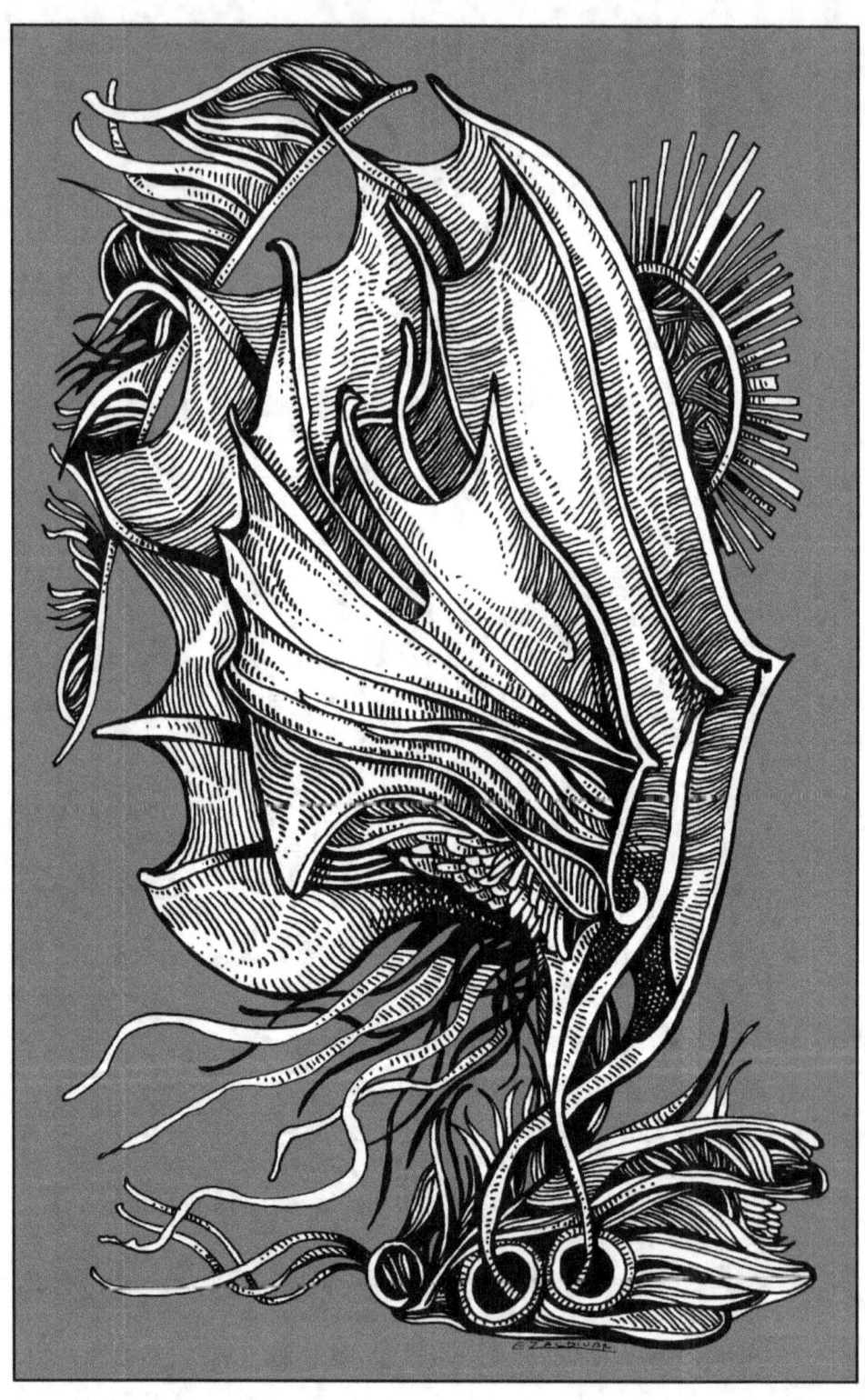

Fallen Angel

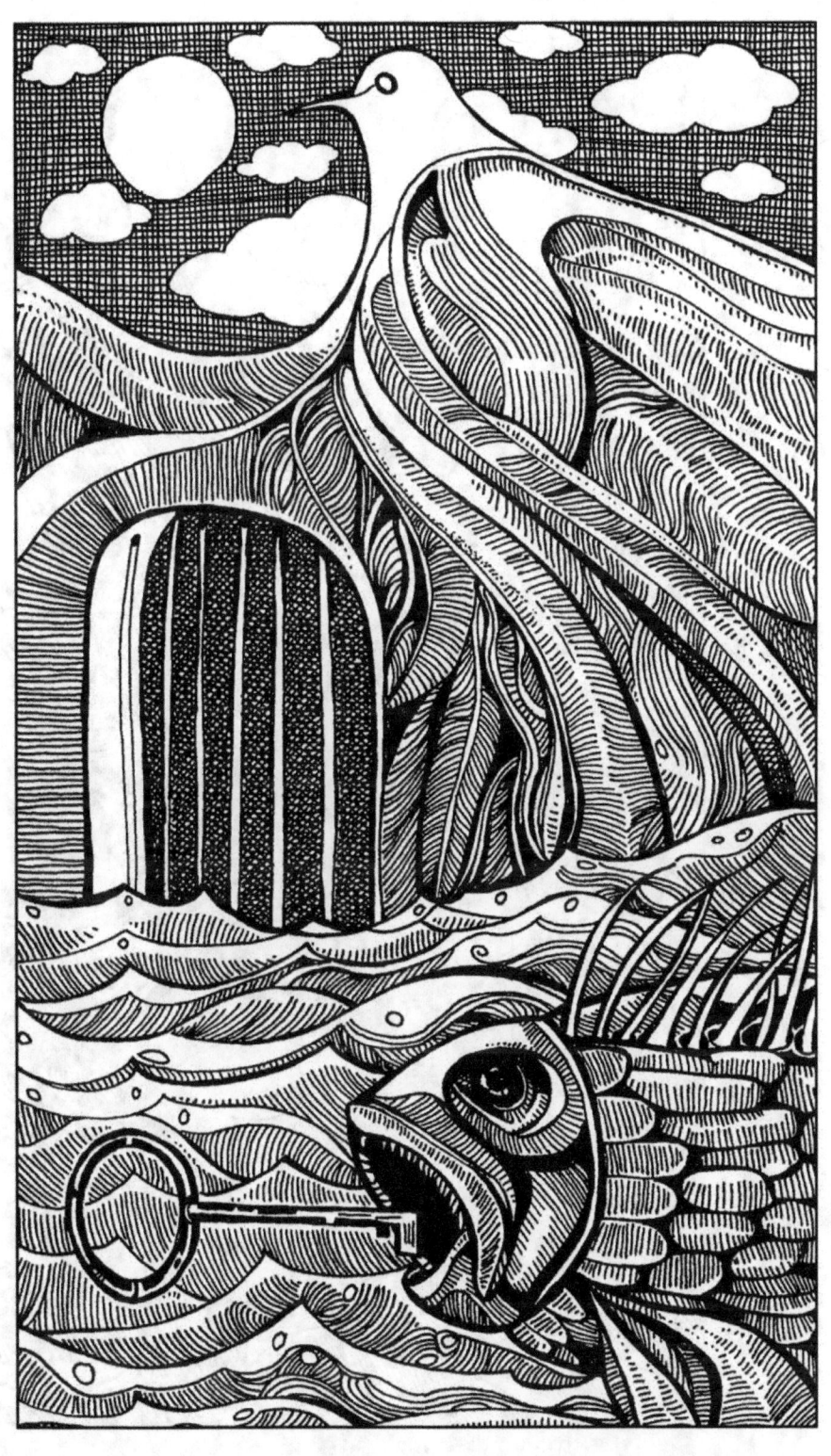

Spiral of paradoxes

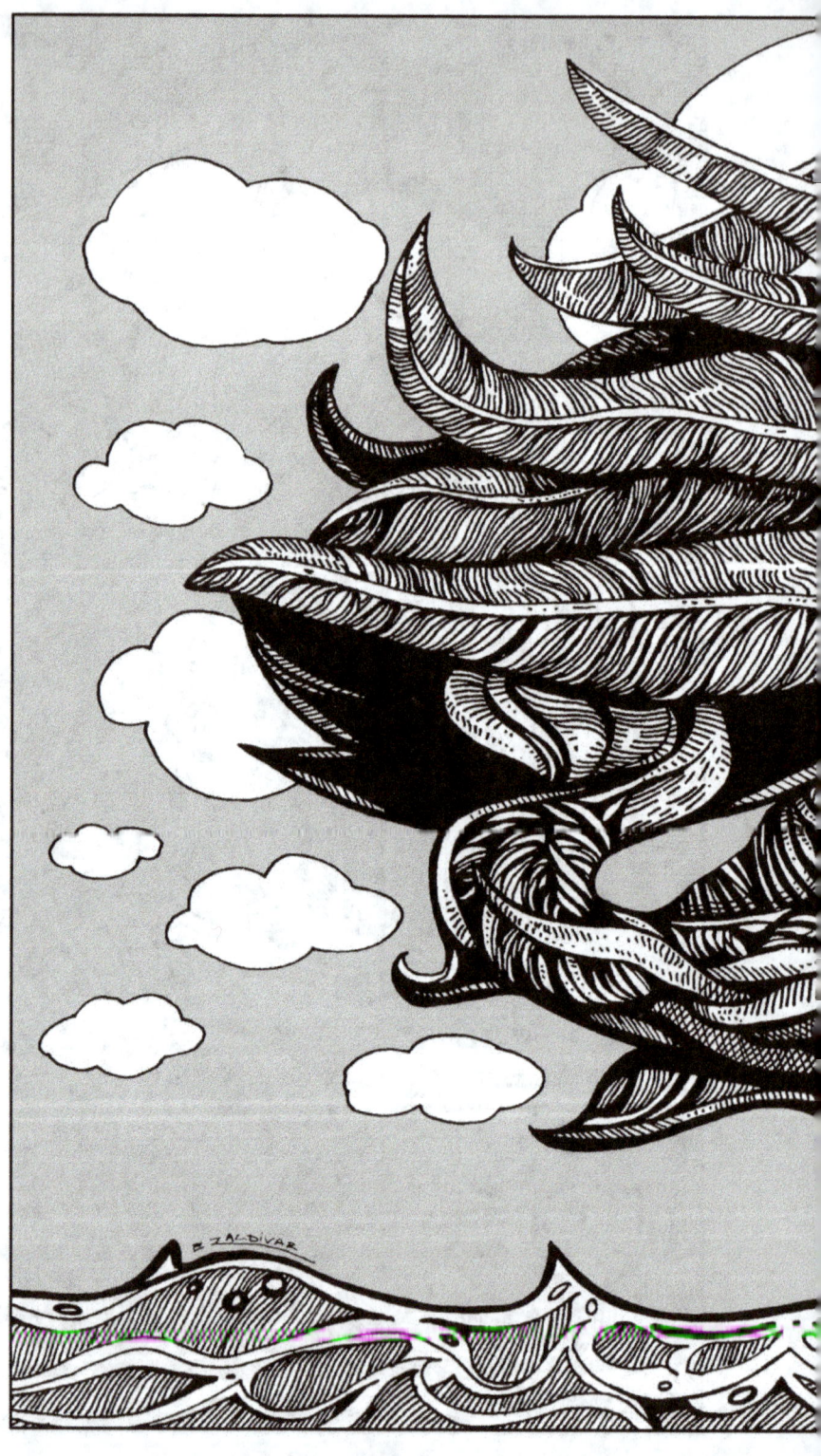

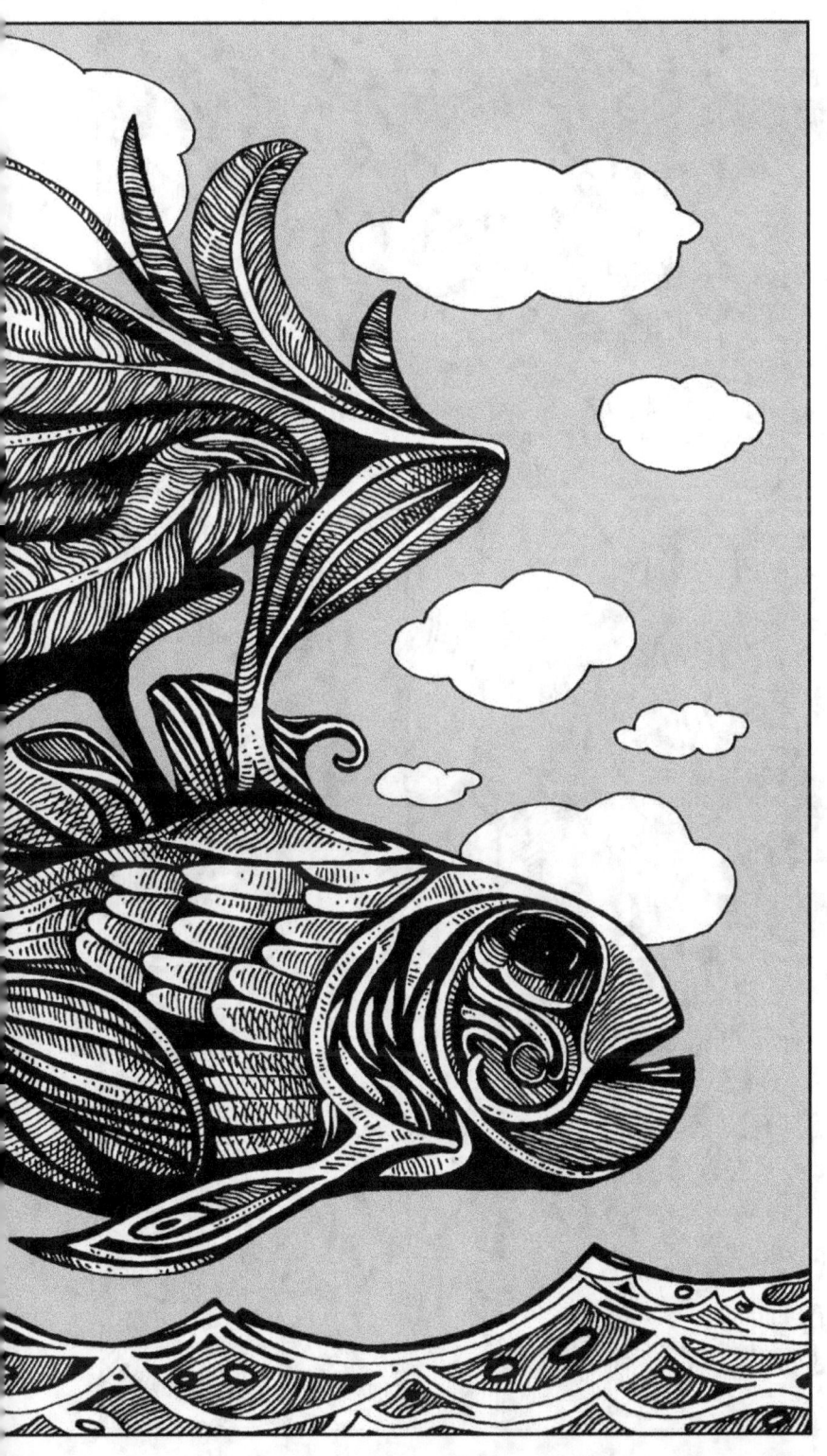

All fish dream of flying

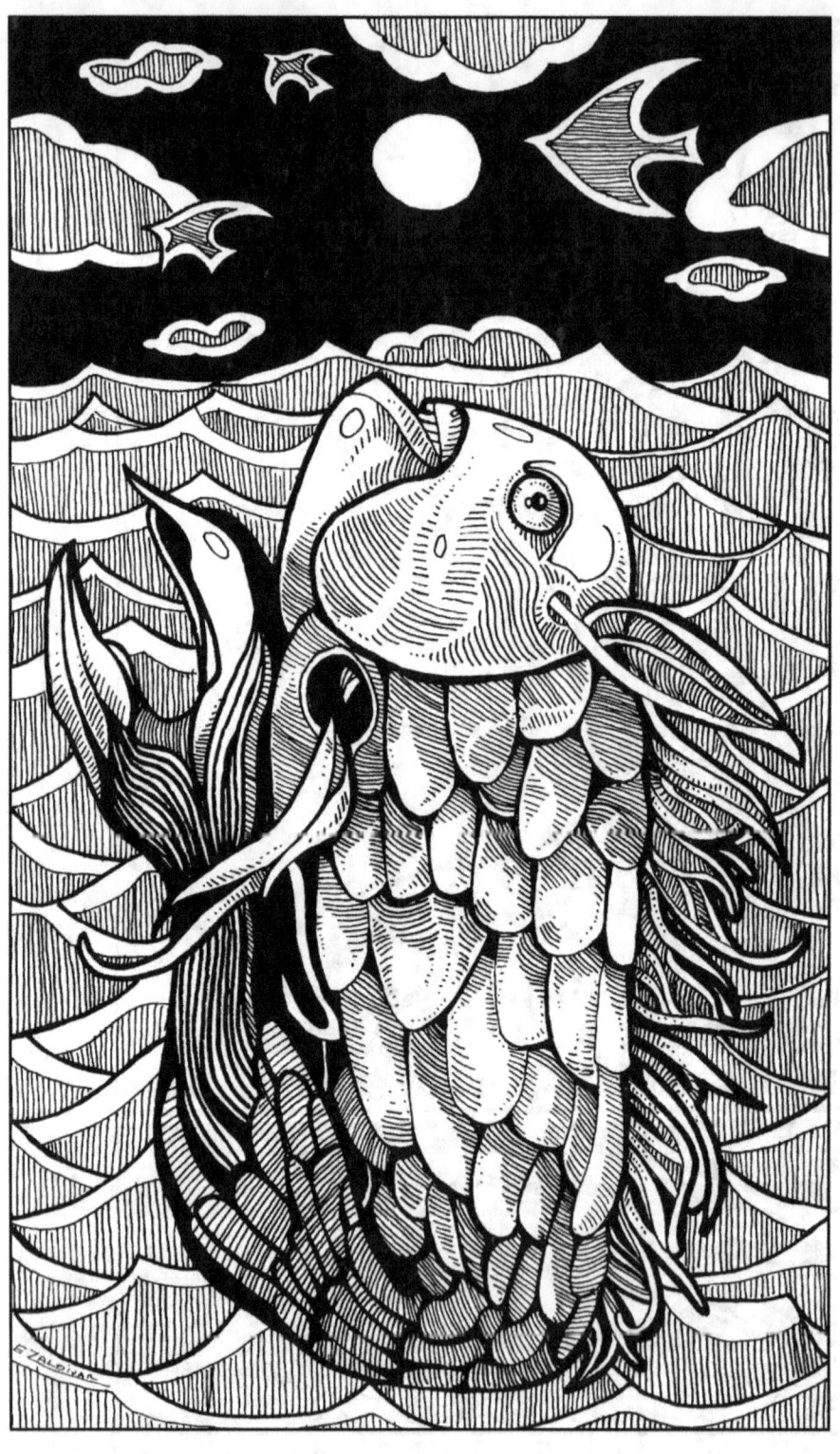

Incongruities

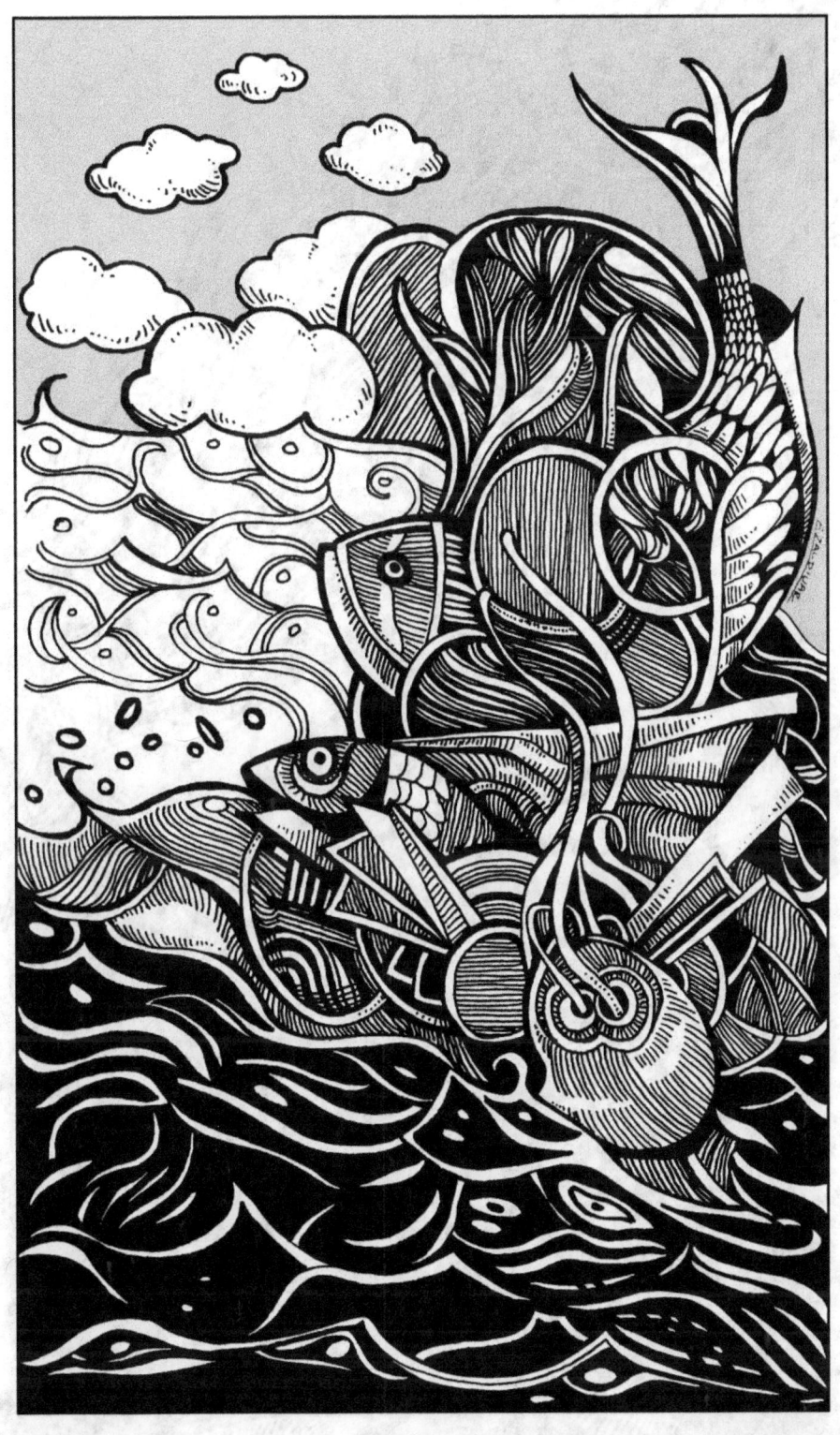

Moved by the storm

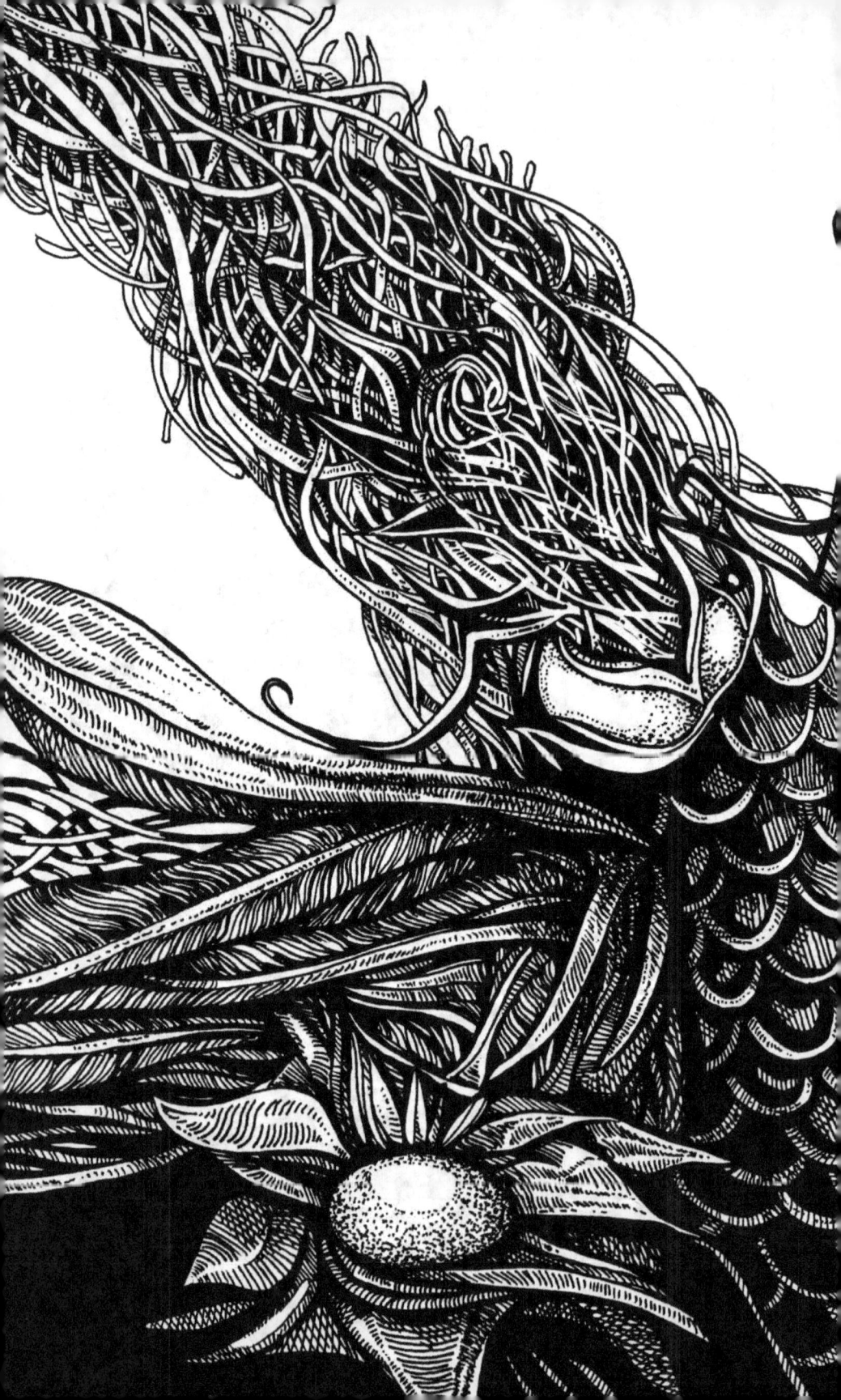

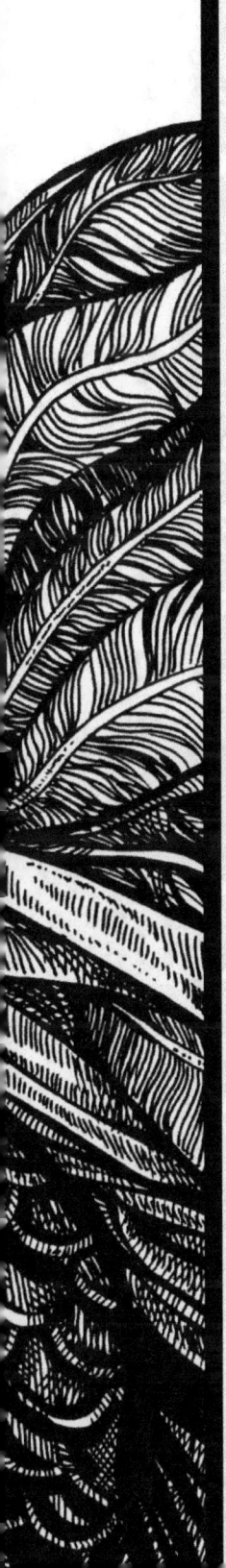

Castaway fish

The trip

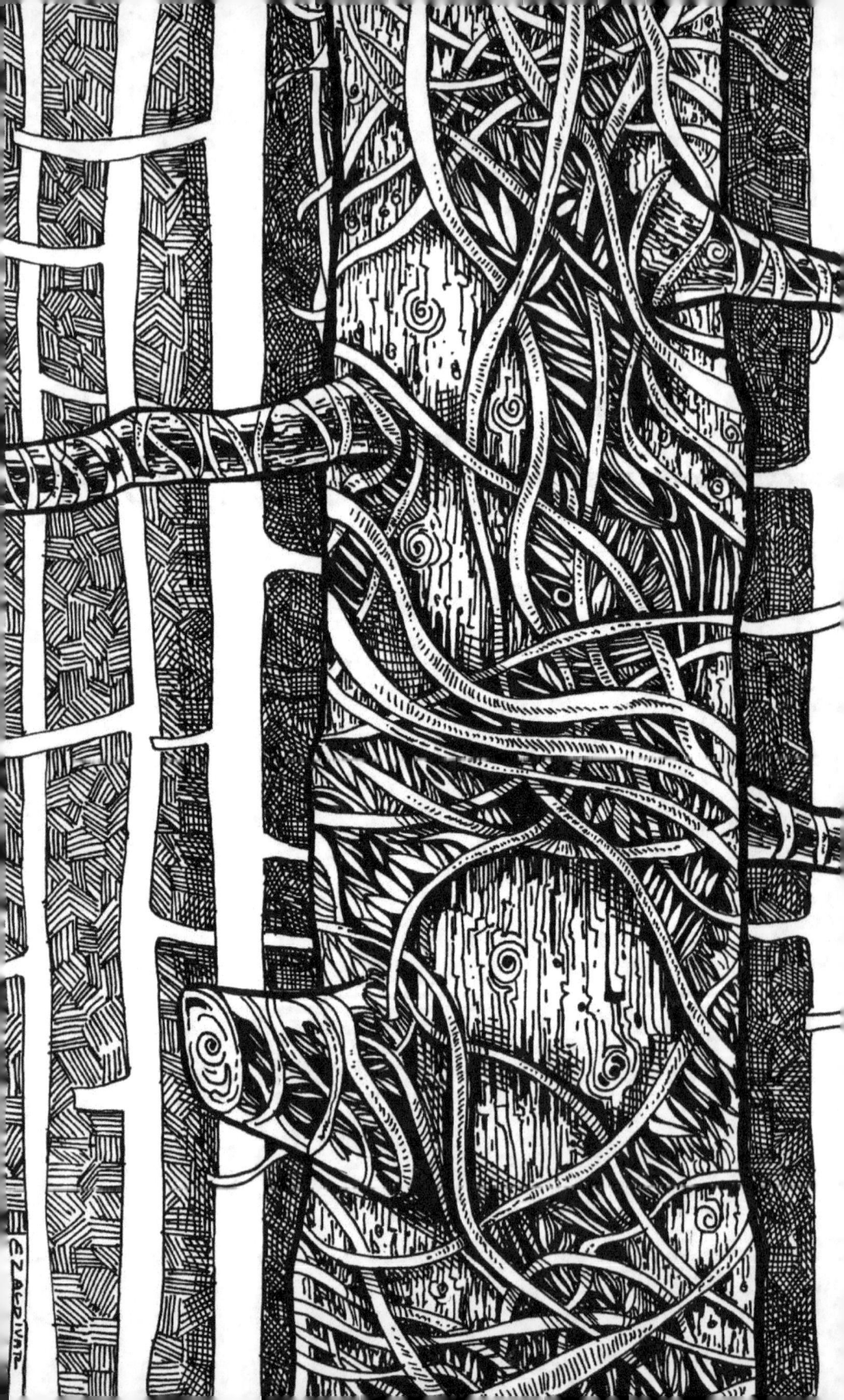

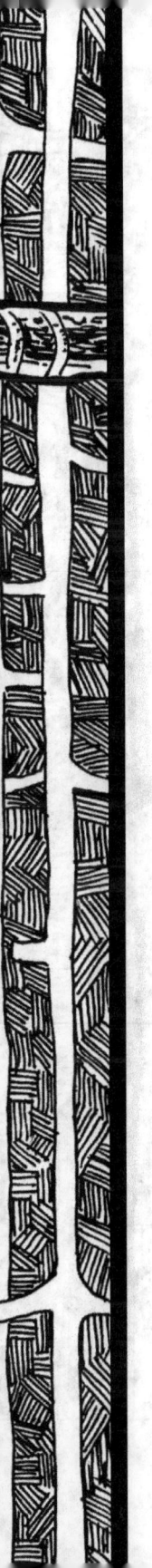

Jungle

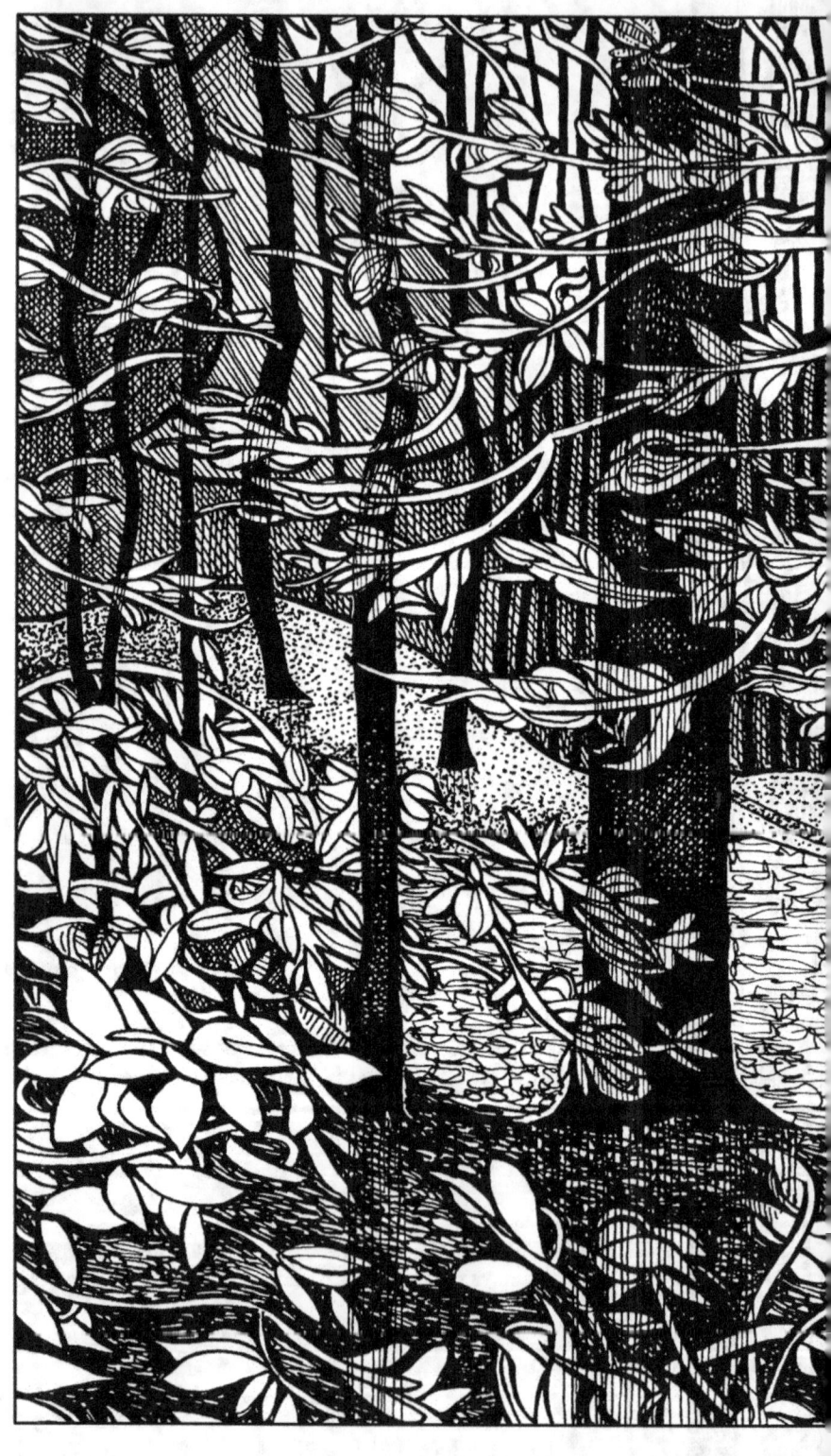

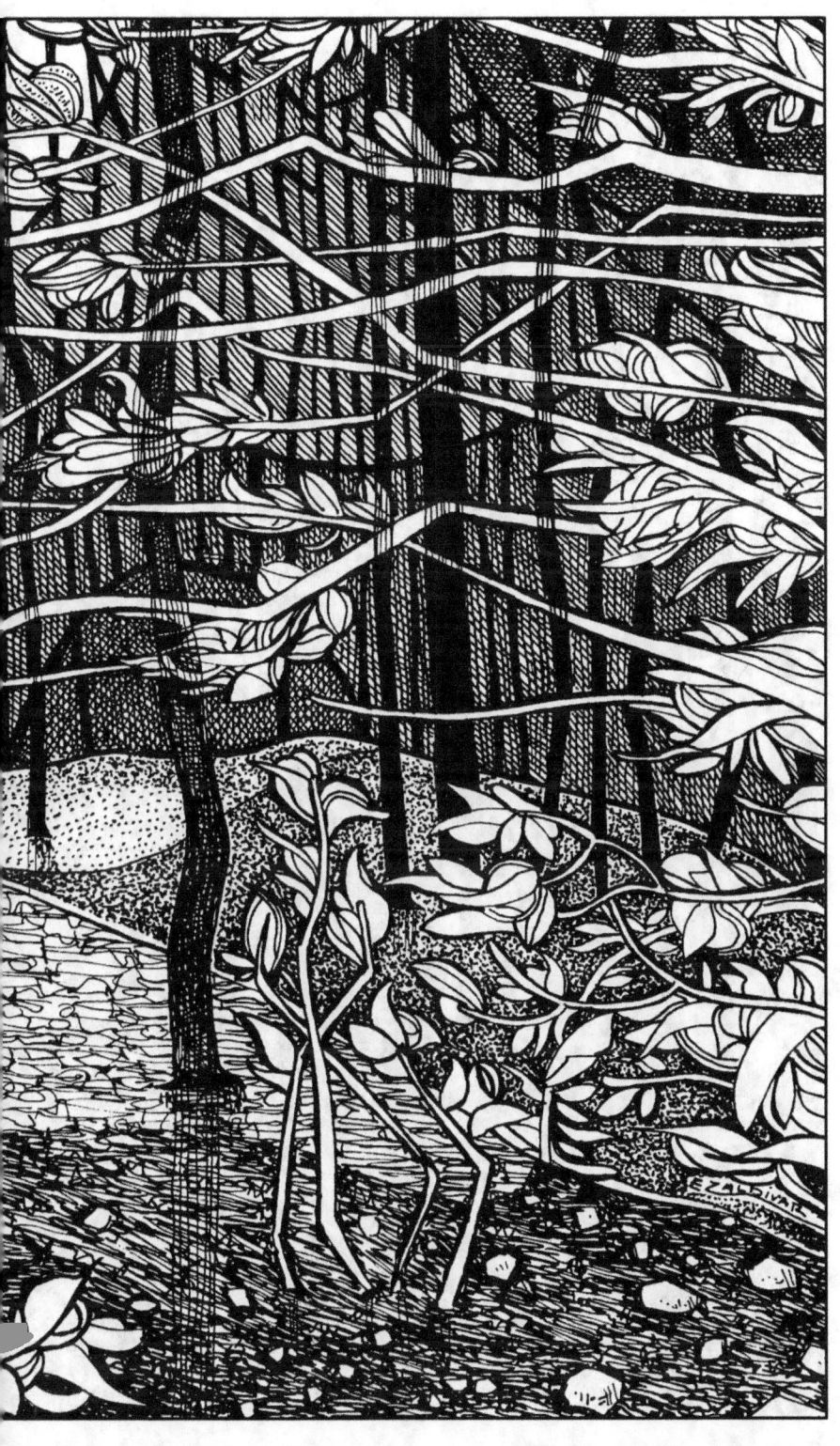

Lost in the forest

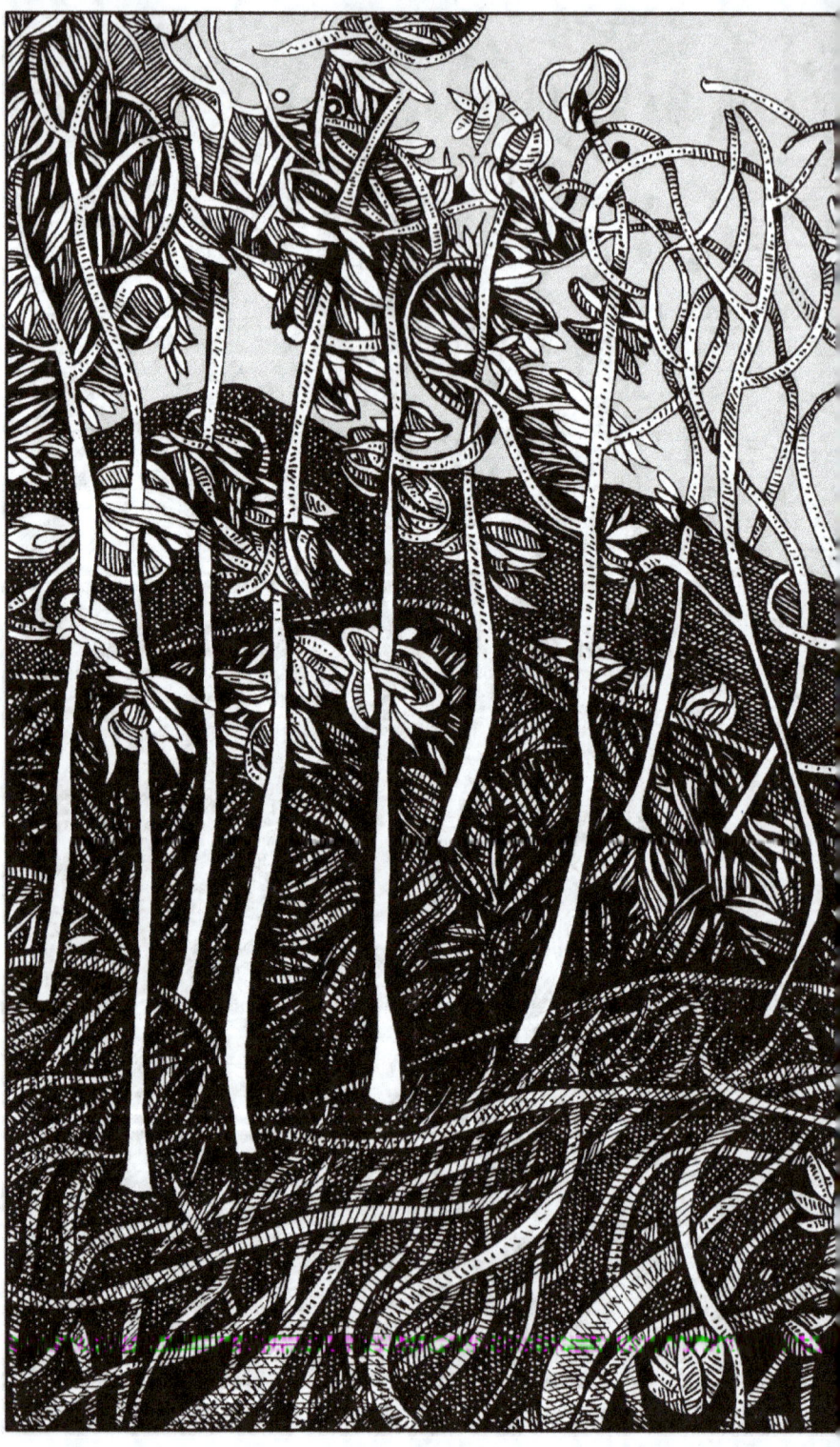

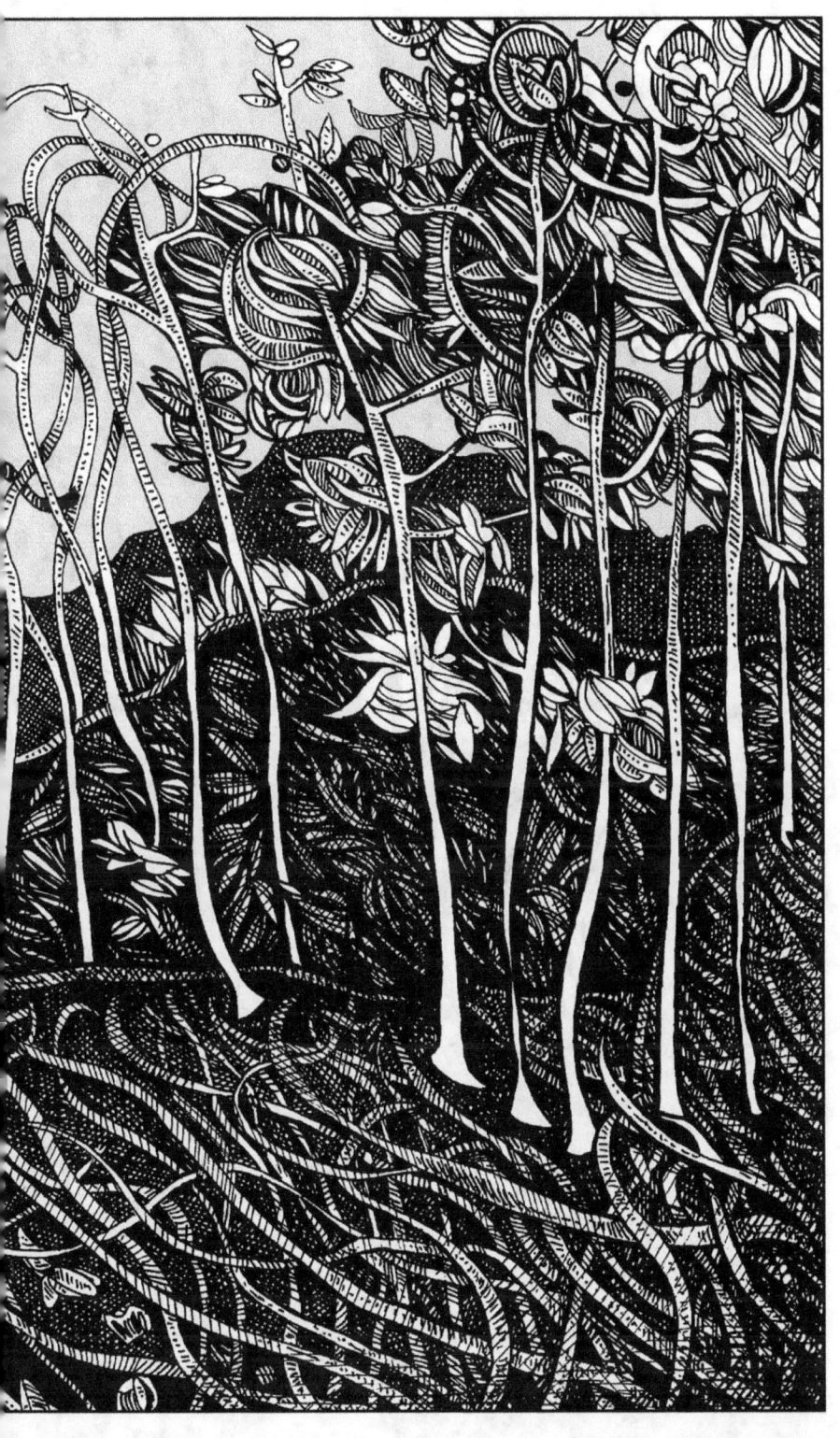

Uncertain horizon

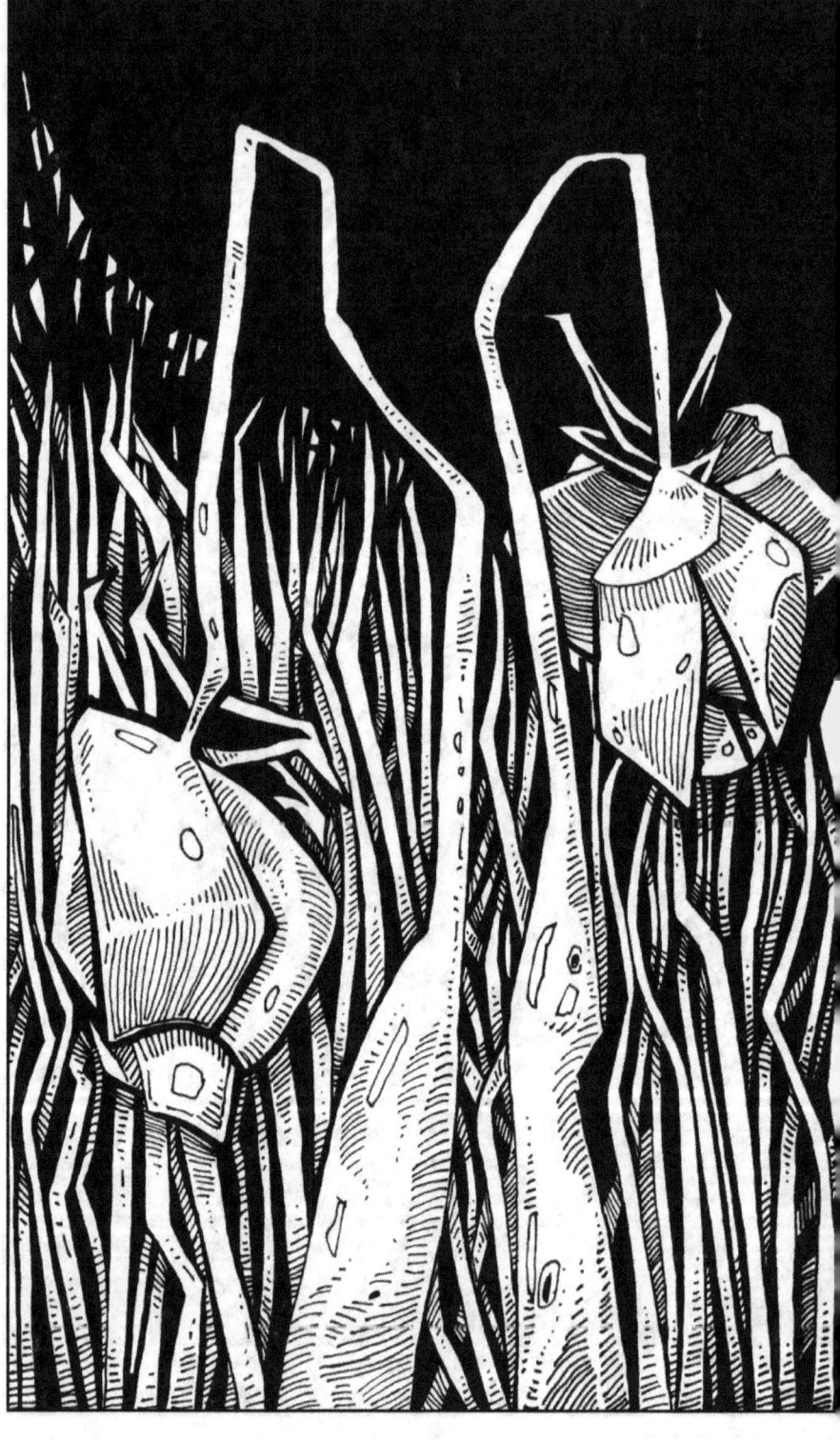

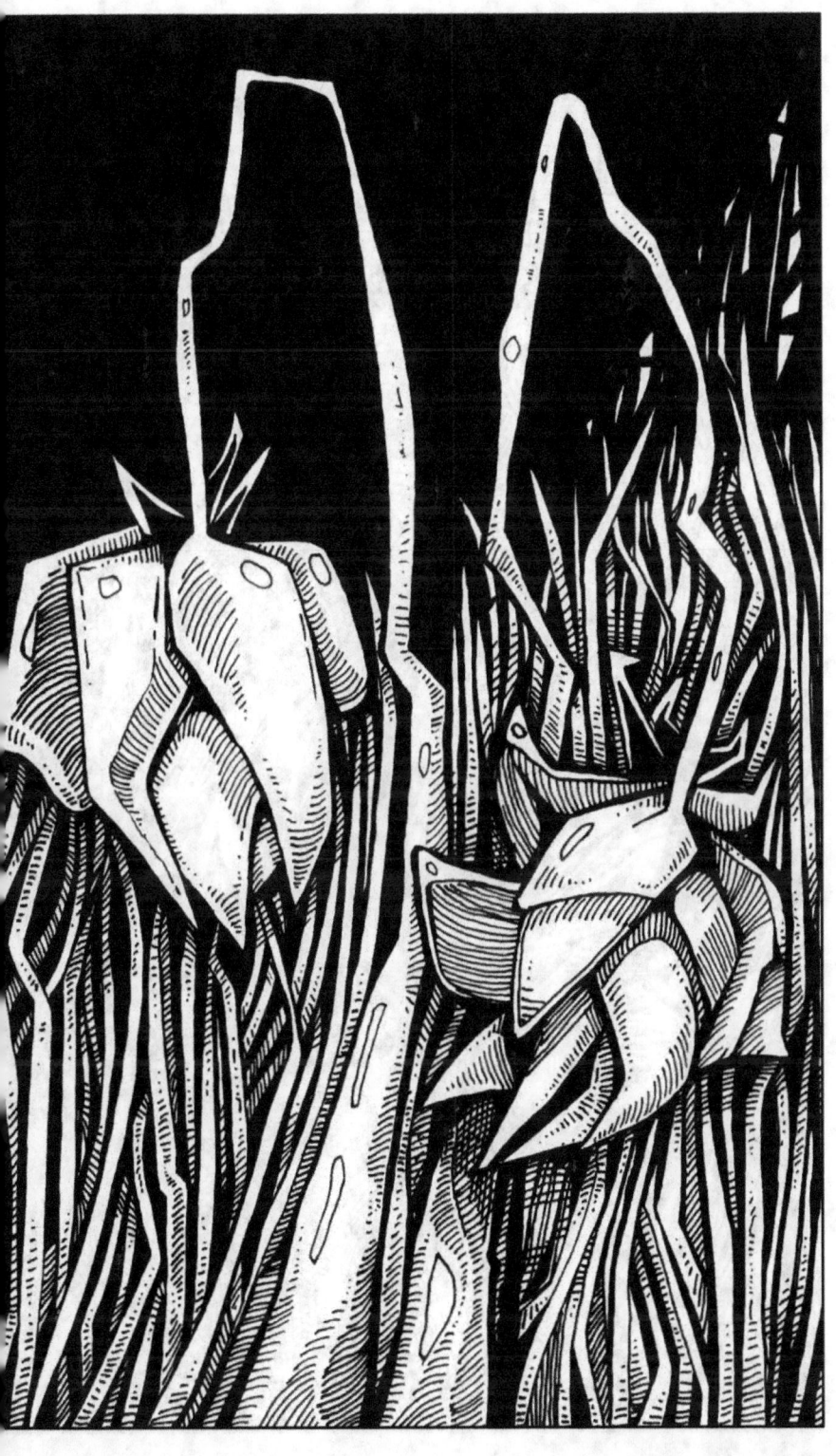

Exotic flowers

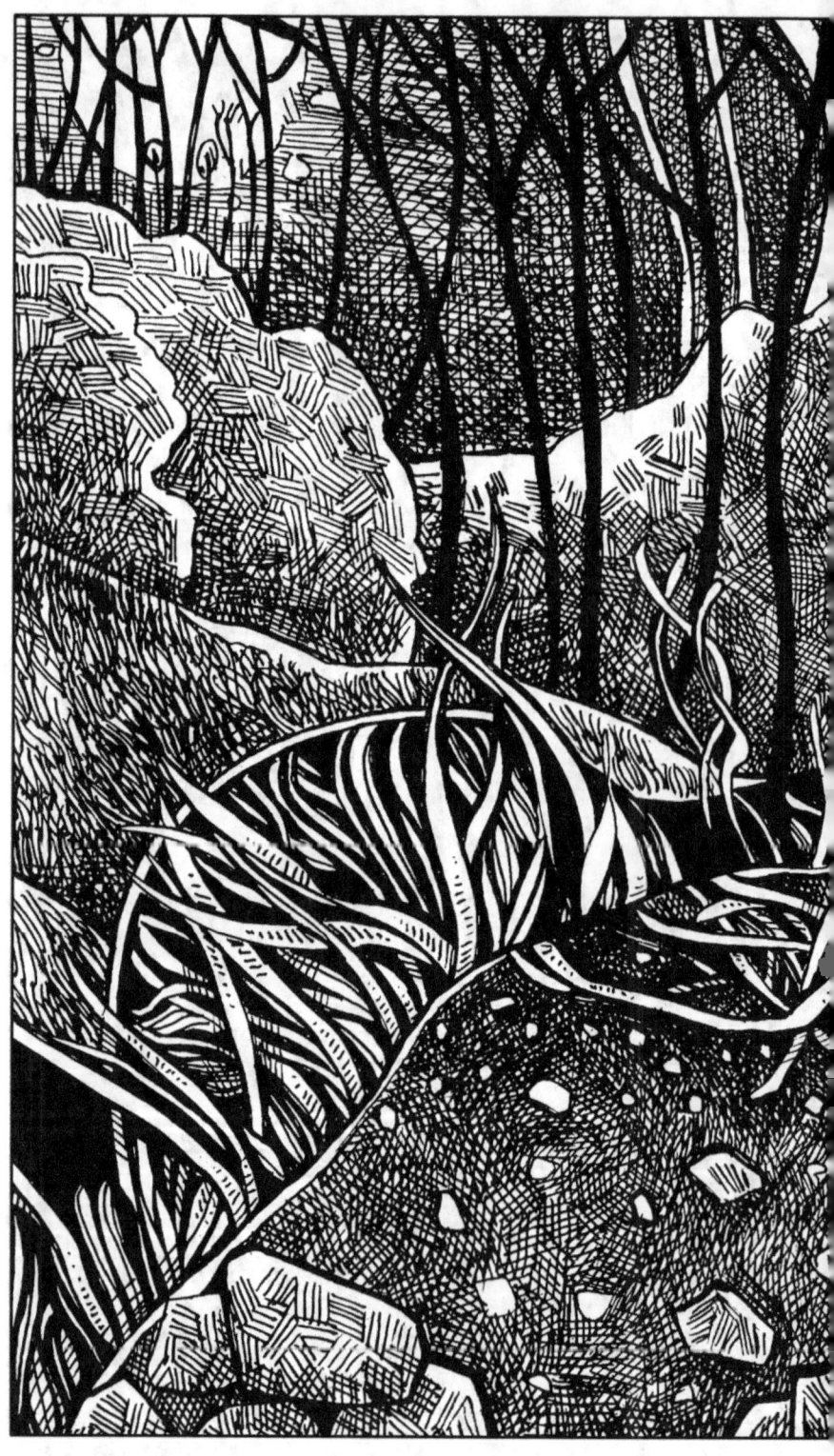

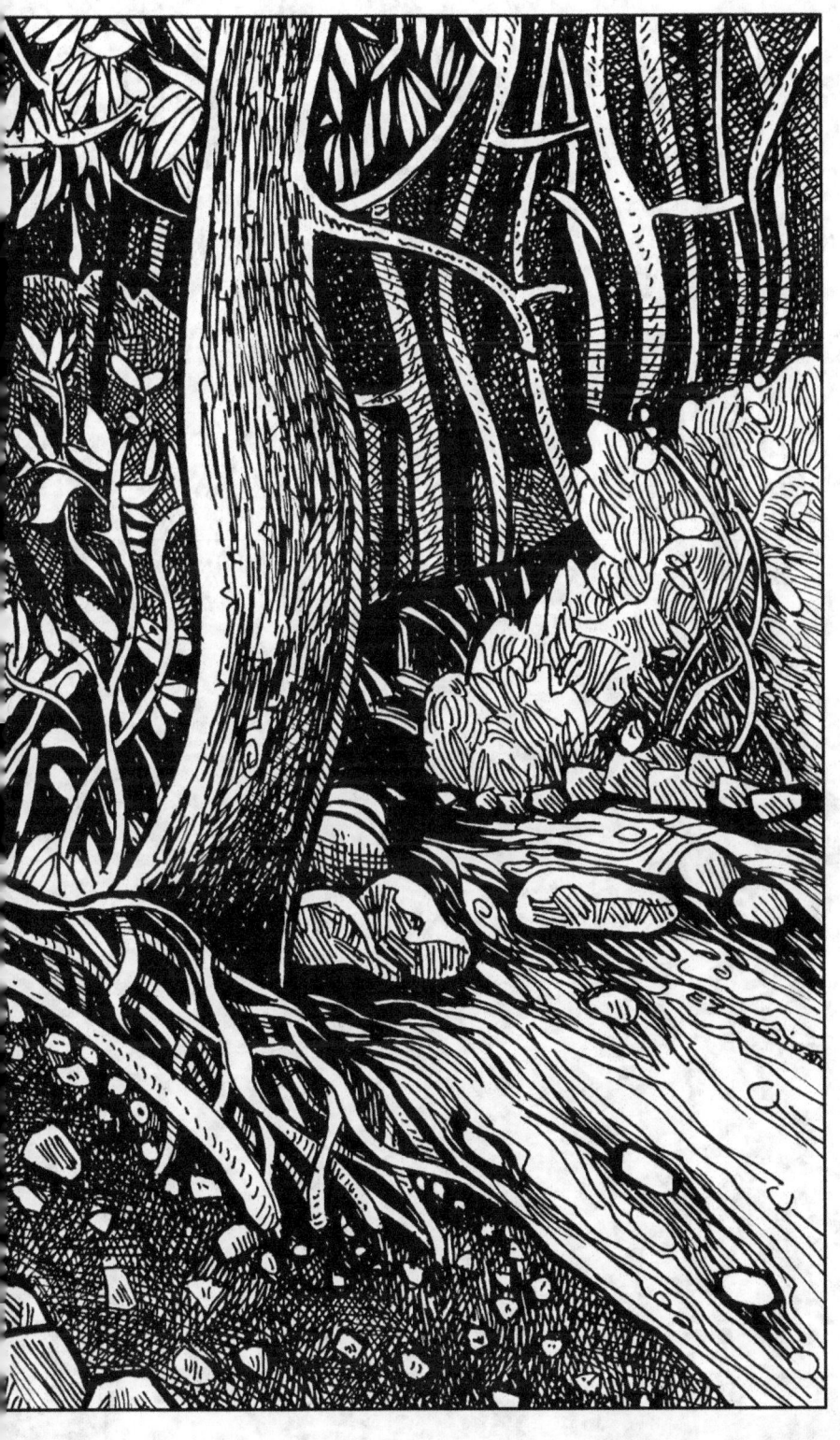

Hints of light

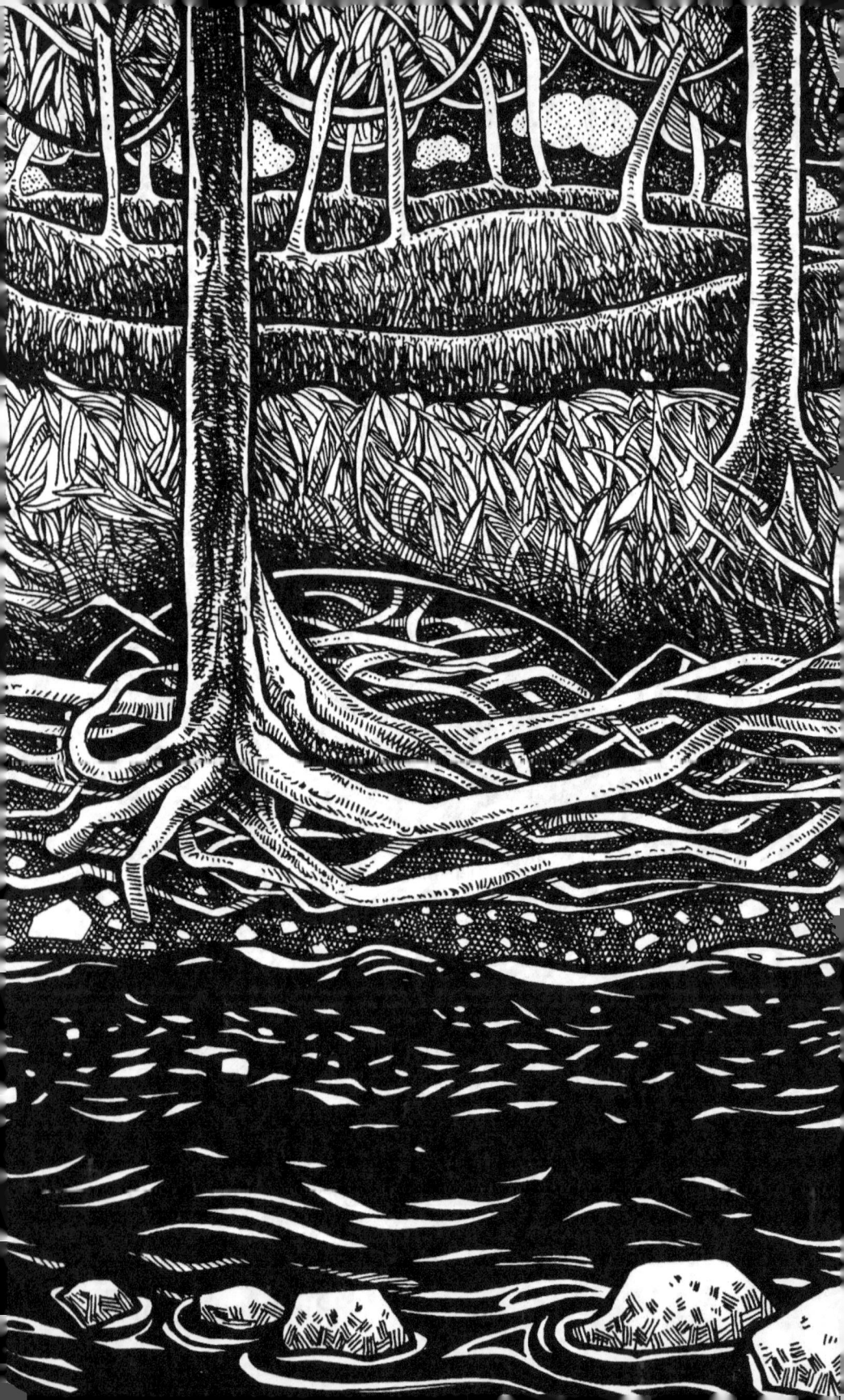

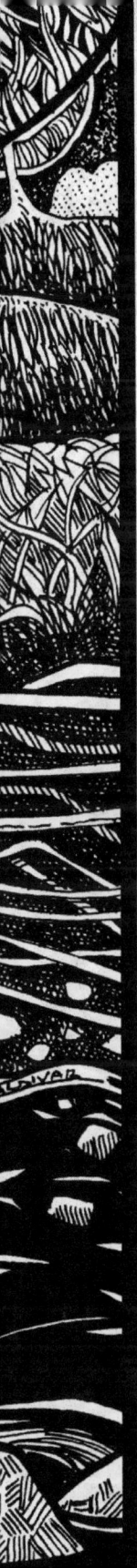

The course of waters

Idyllic landscape

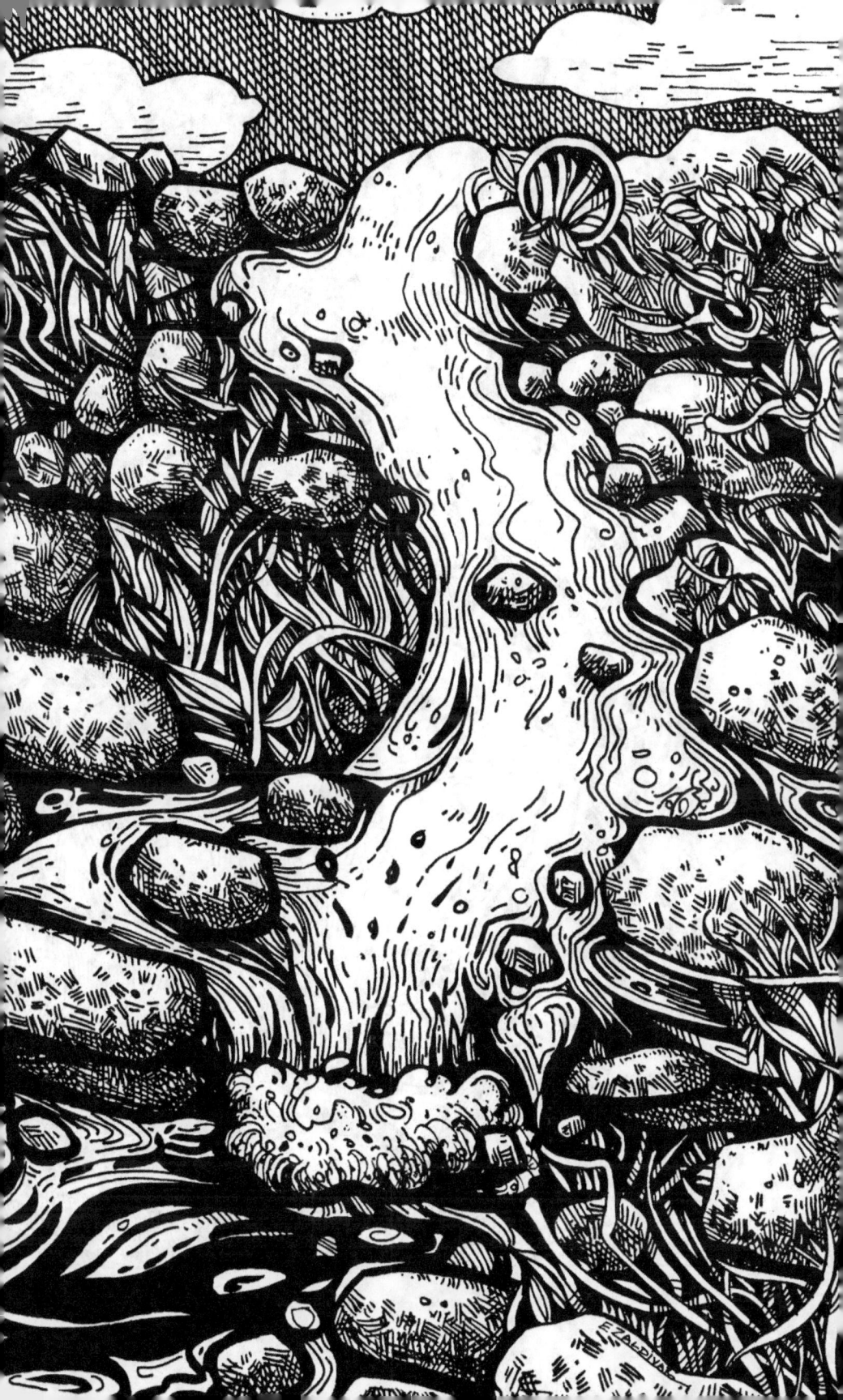

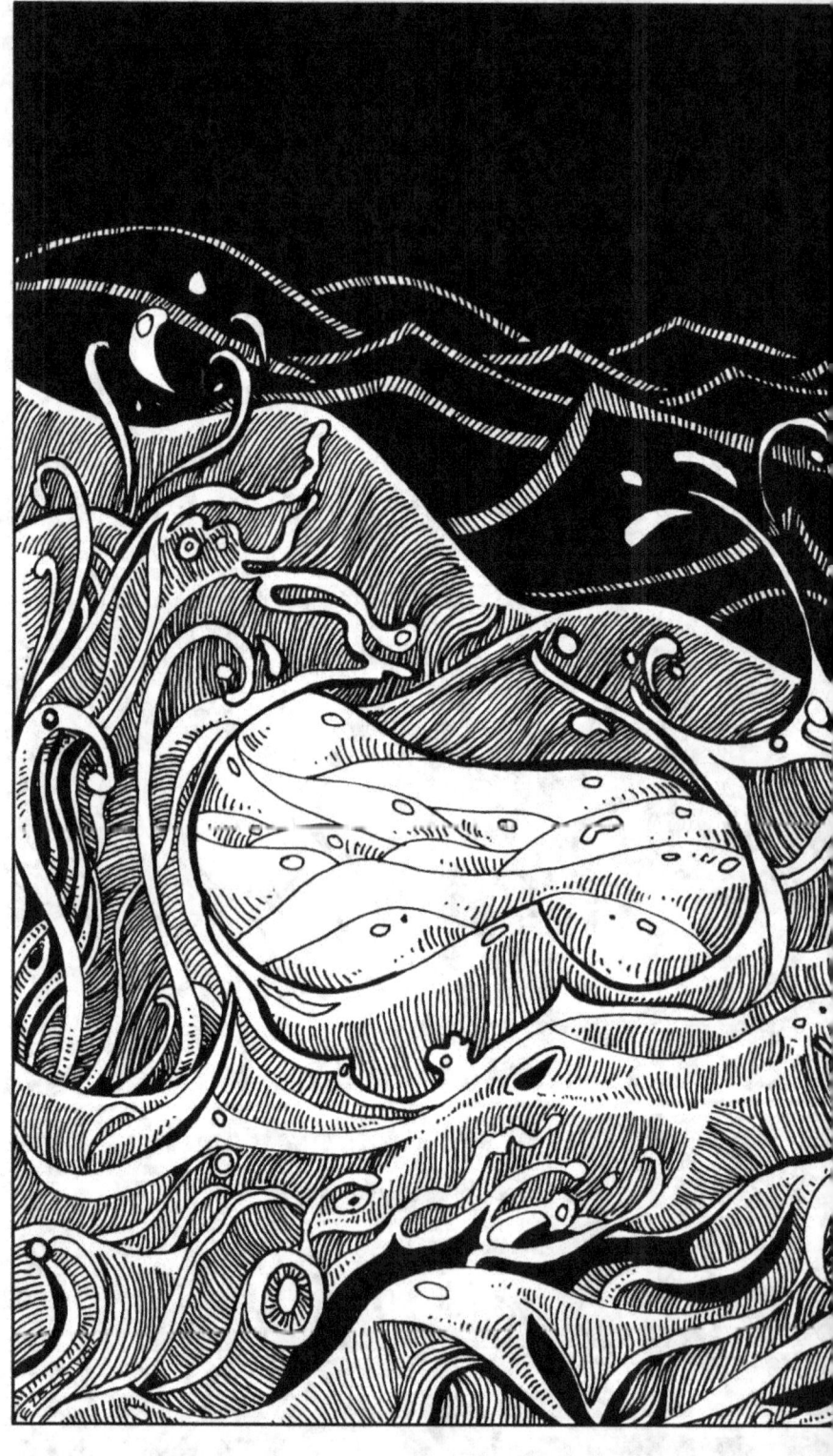

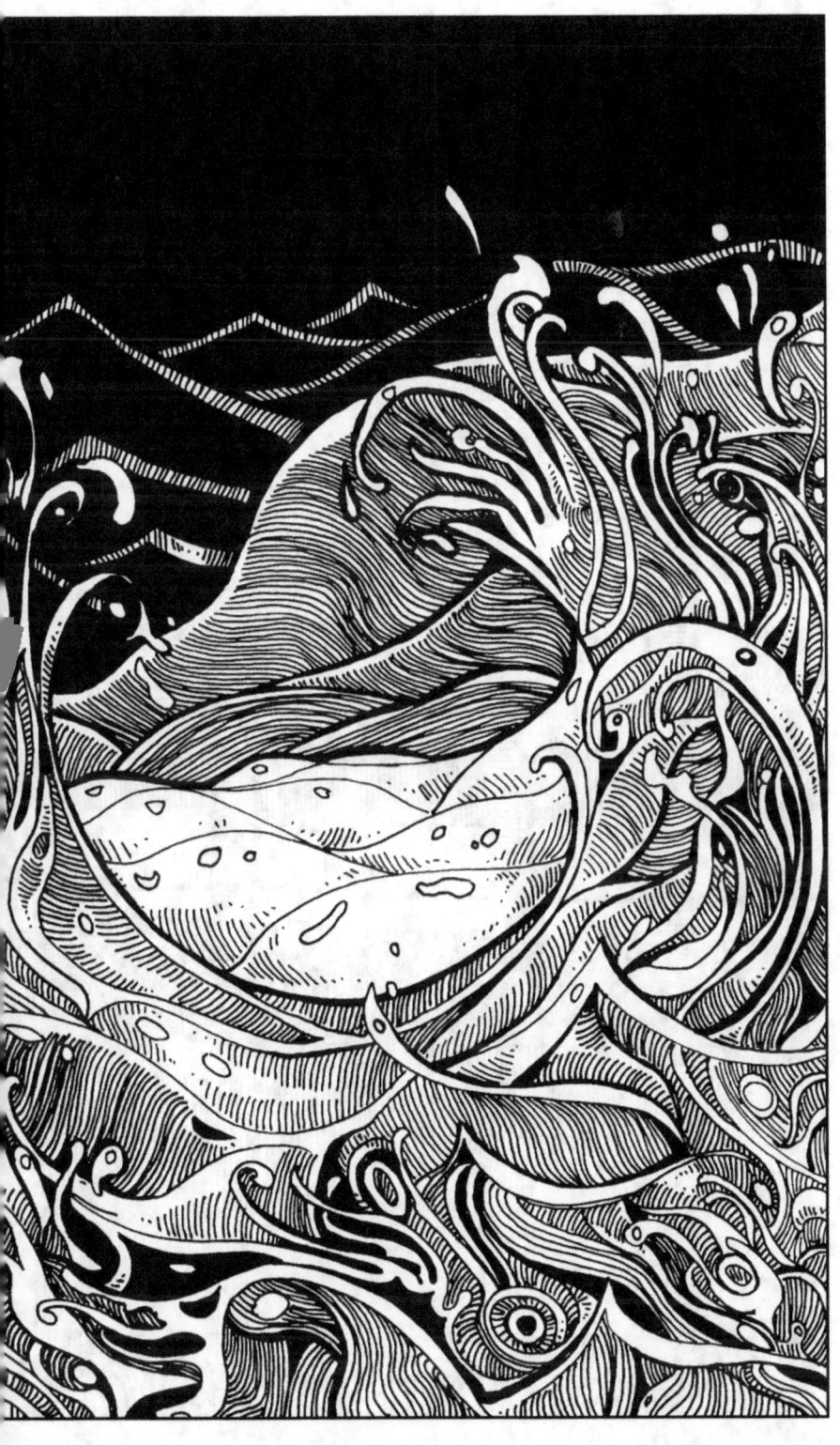

Restless waters

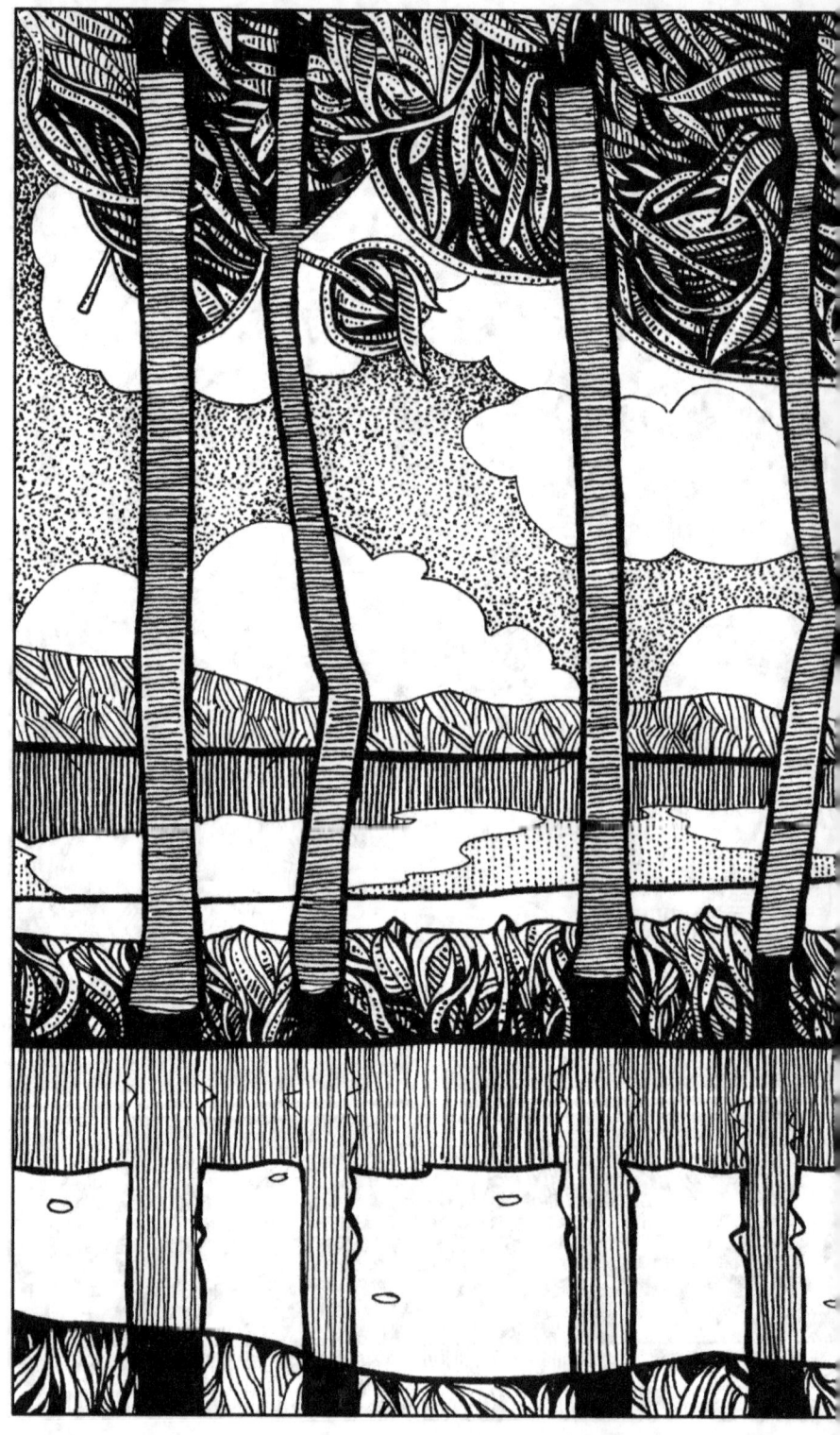

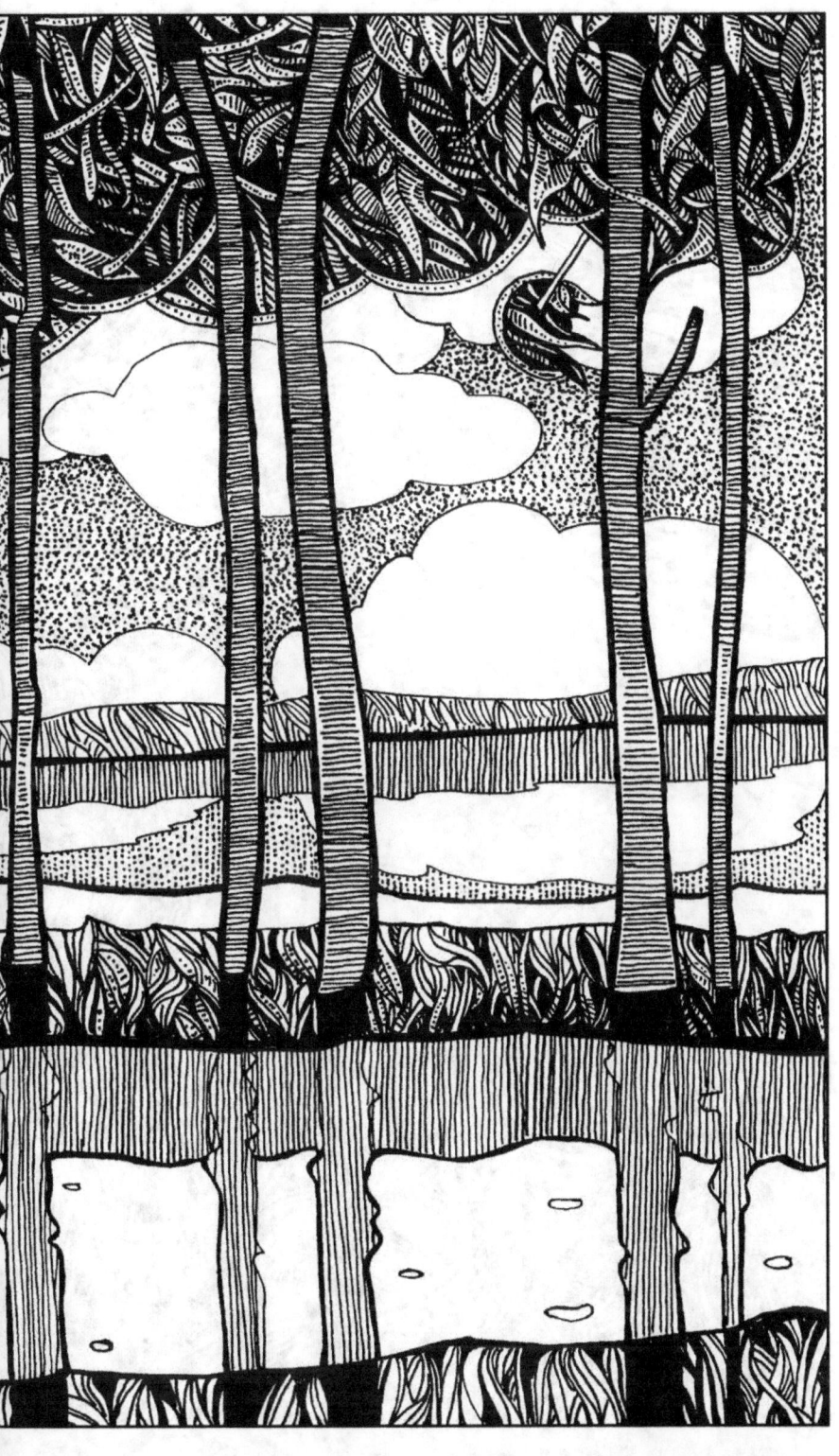

Calm waters

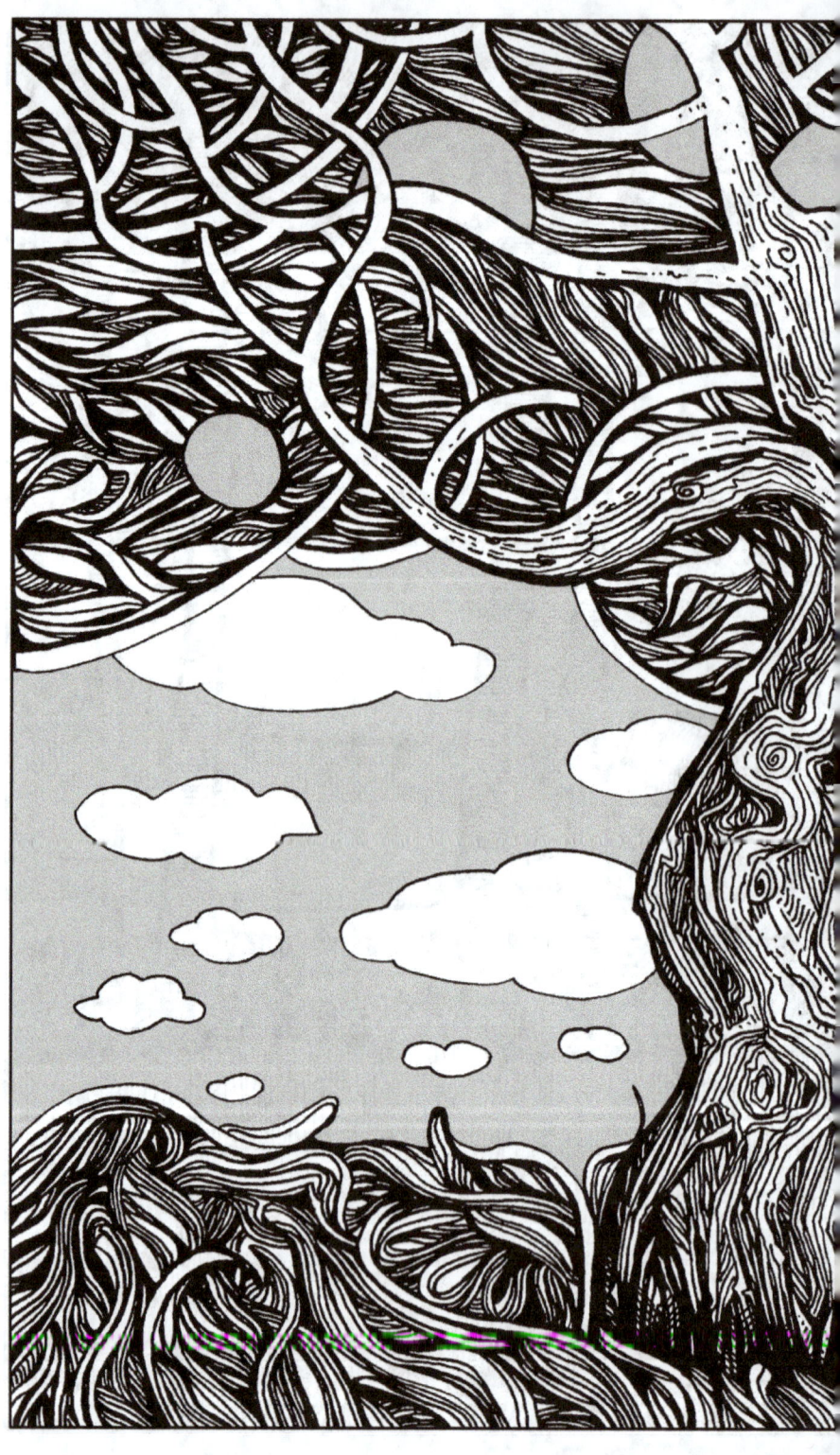

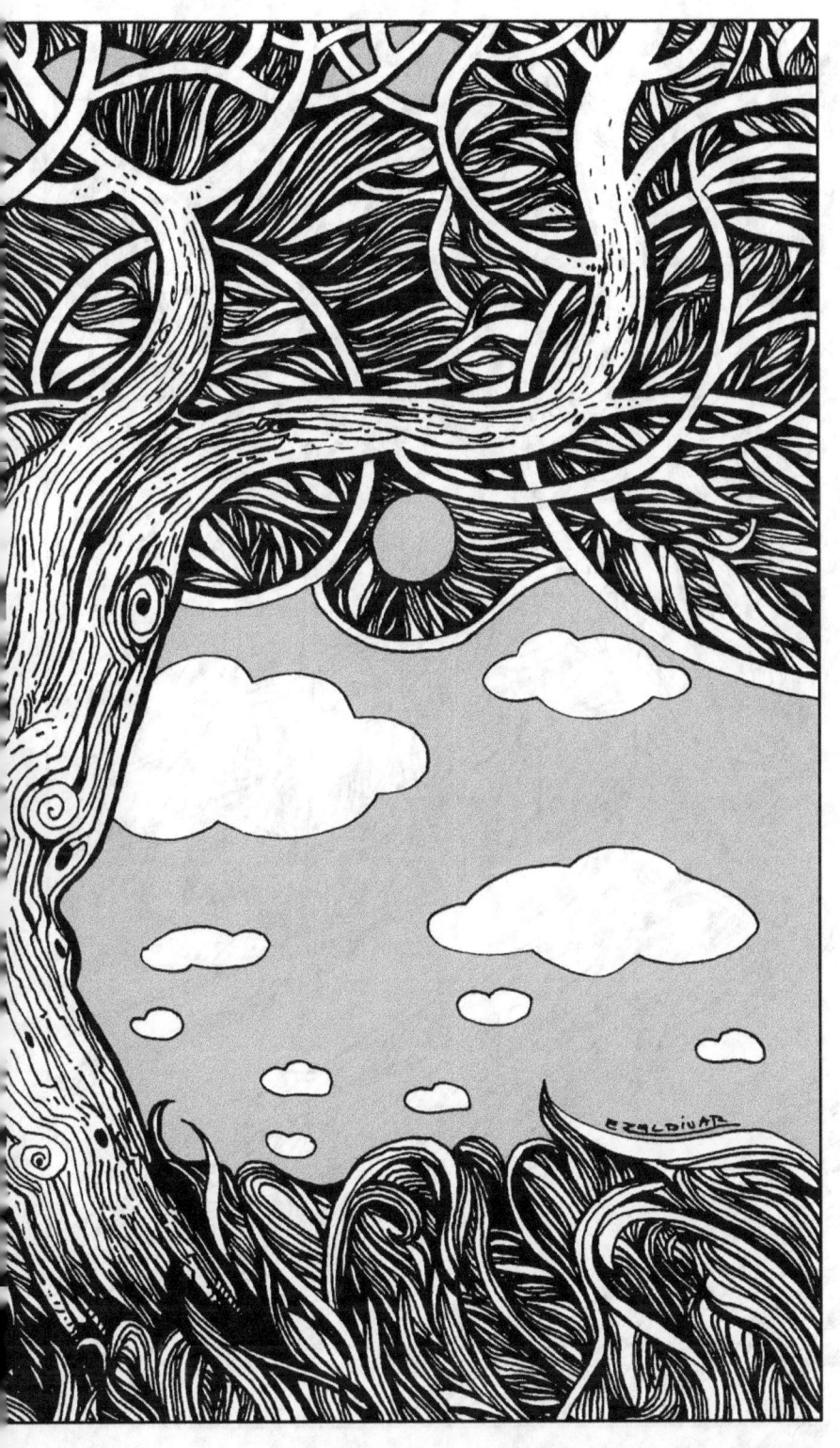

Between heaven and earth

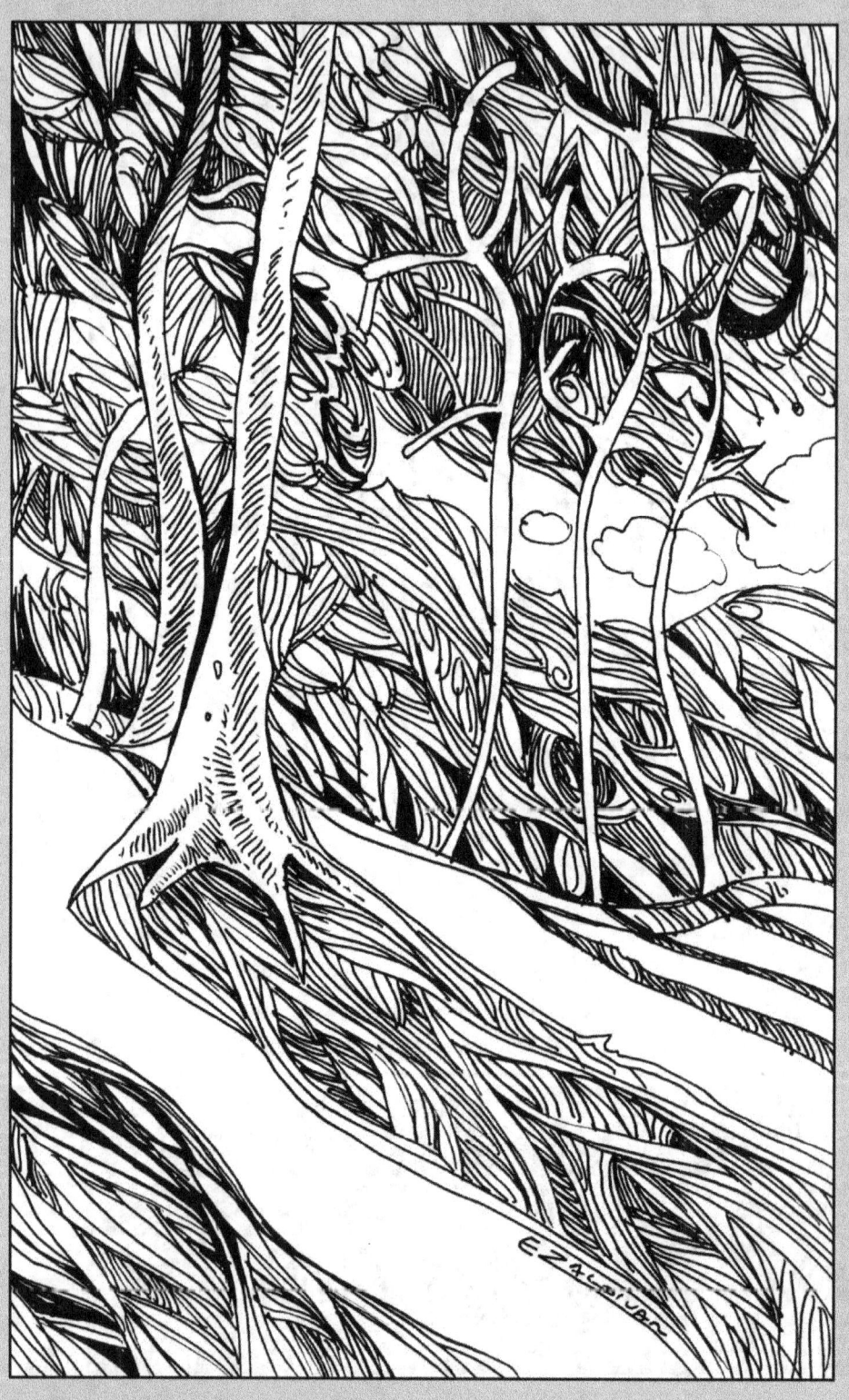

Bathed in light

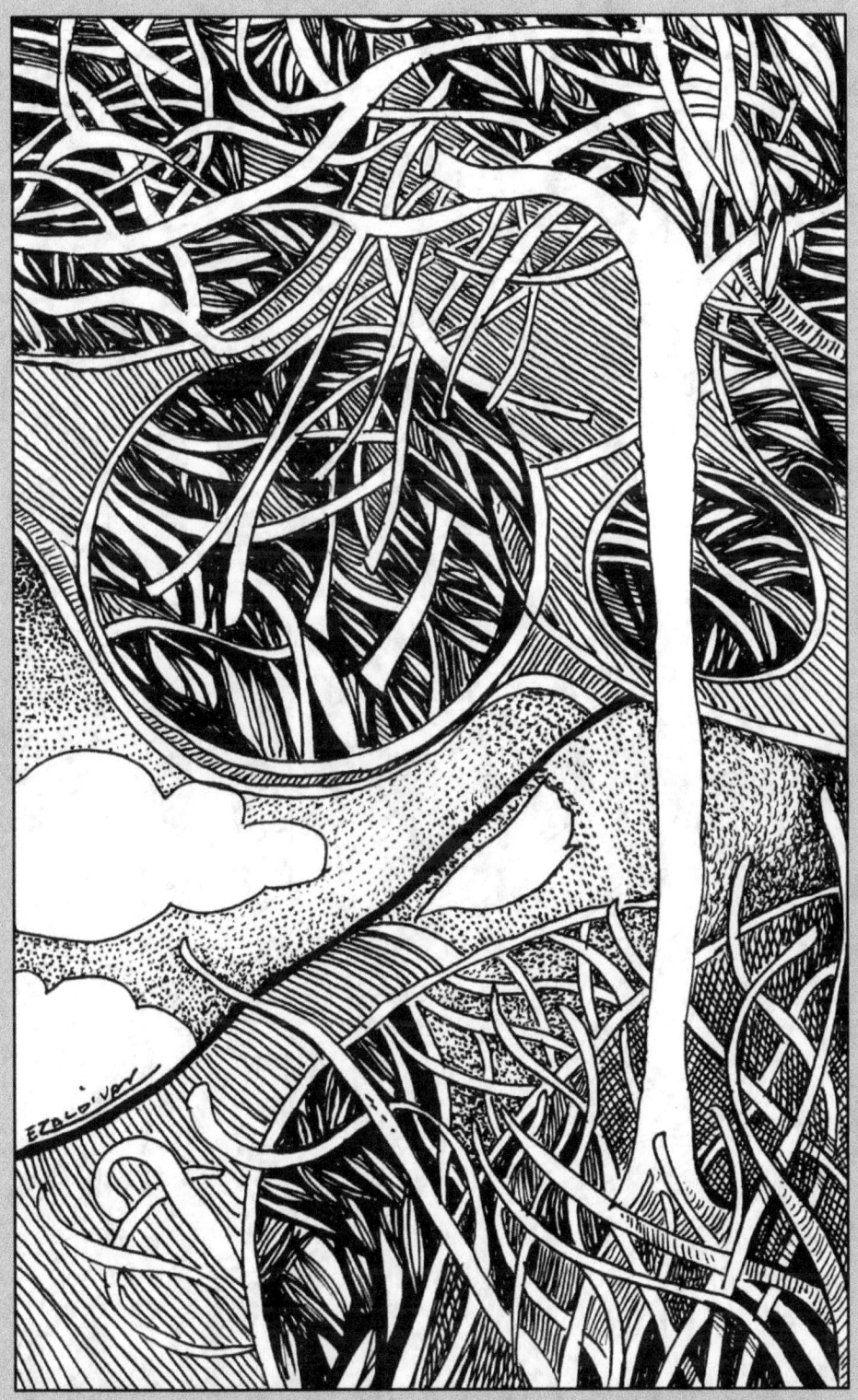

Arbor

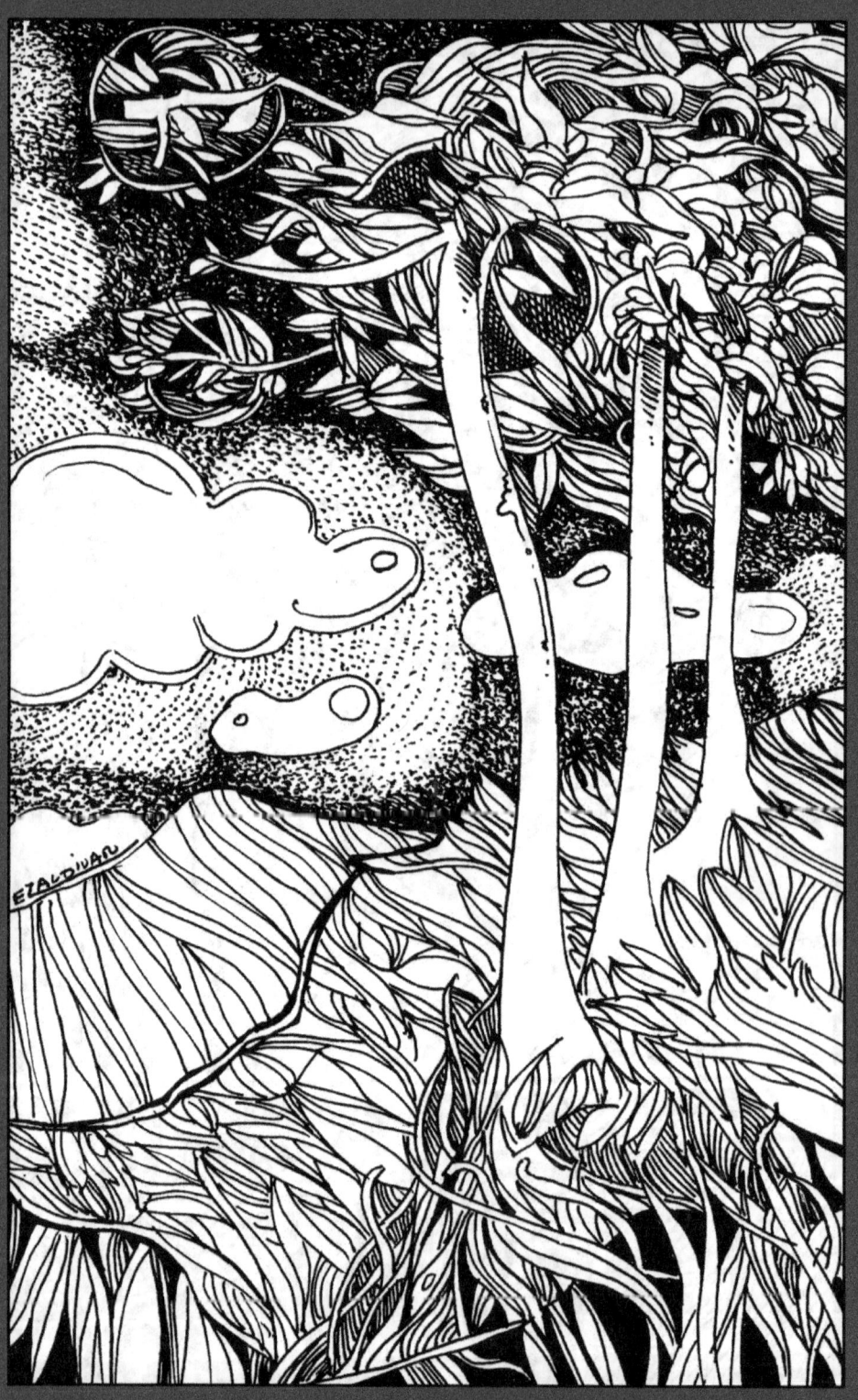

In the middle of the mountain

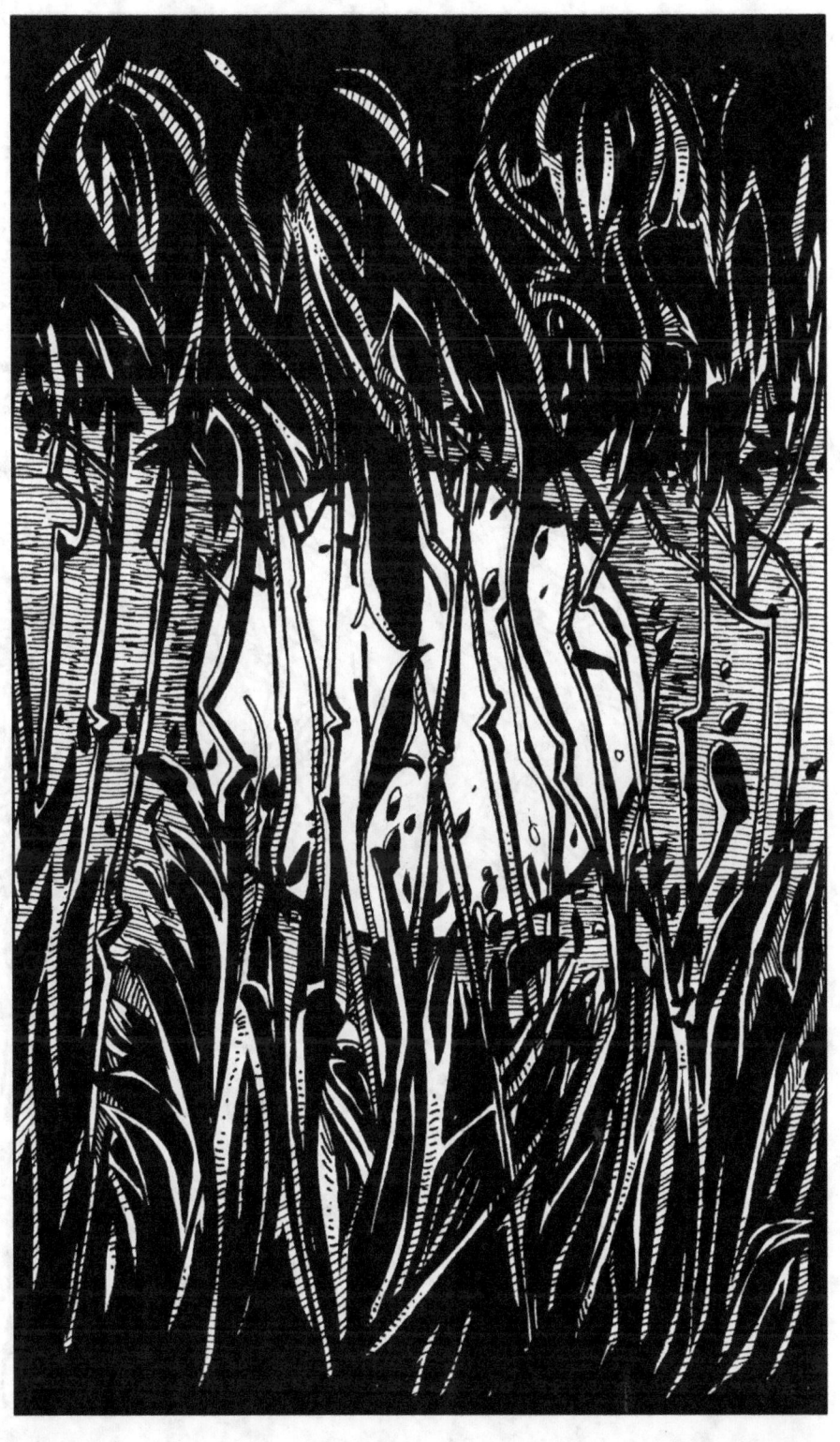

Twilight

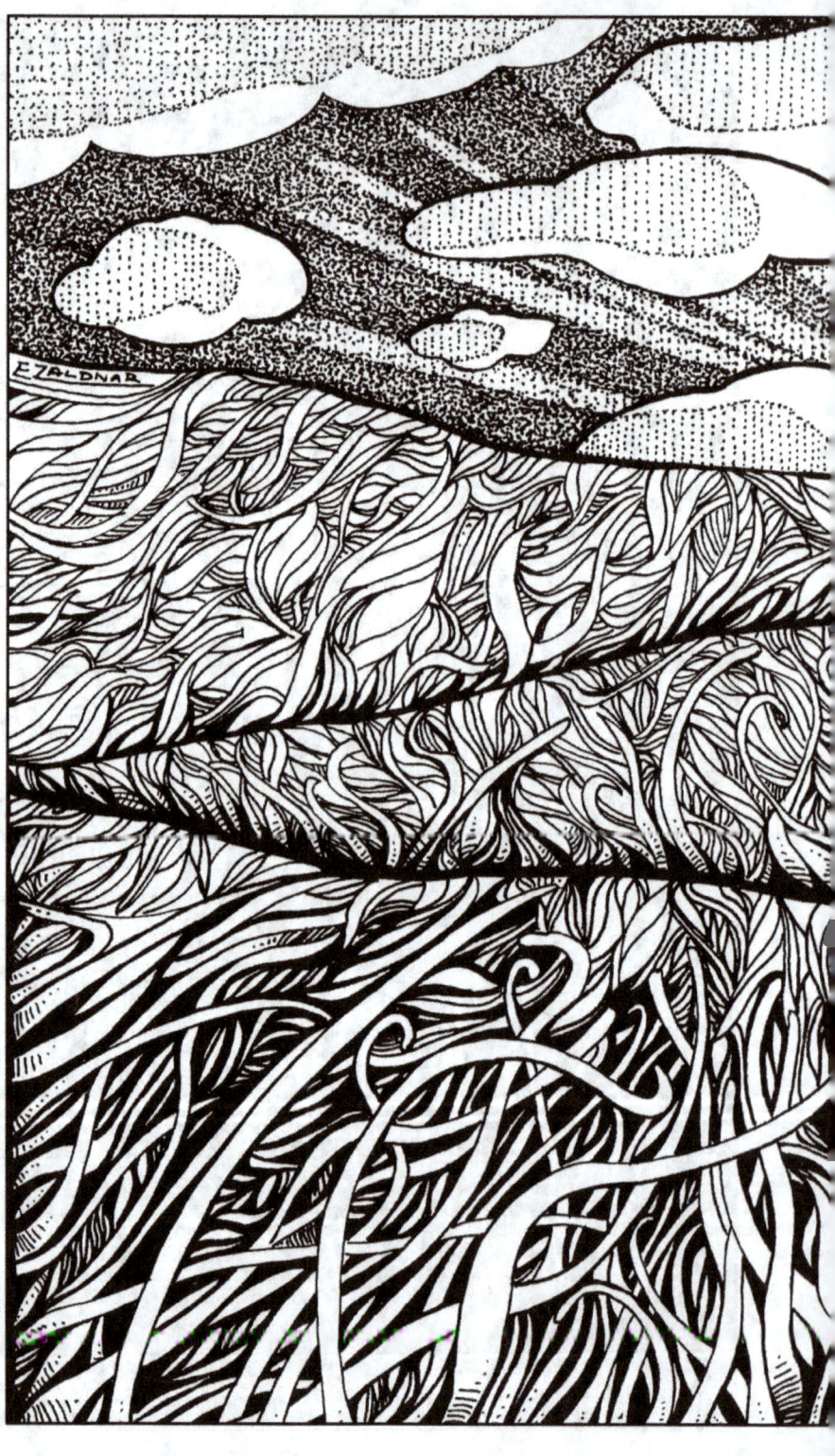

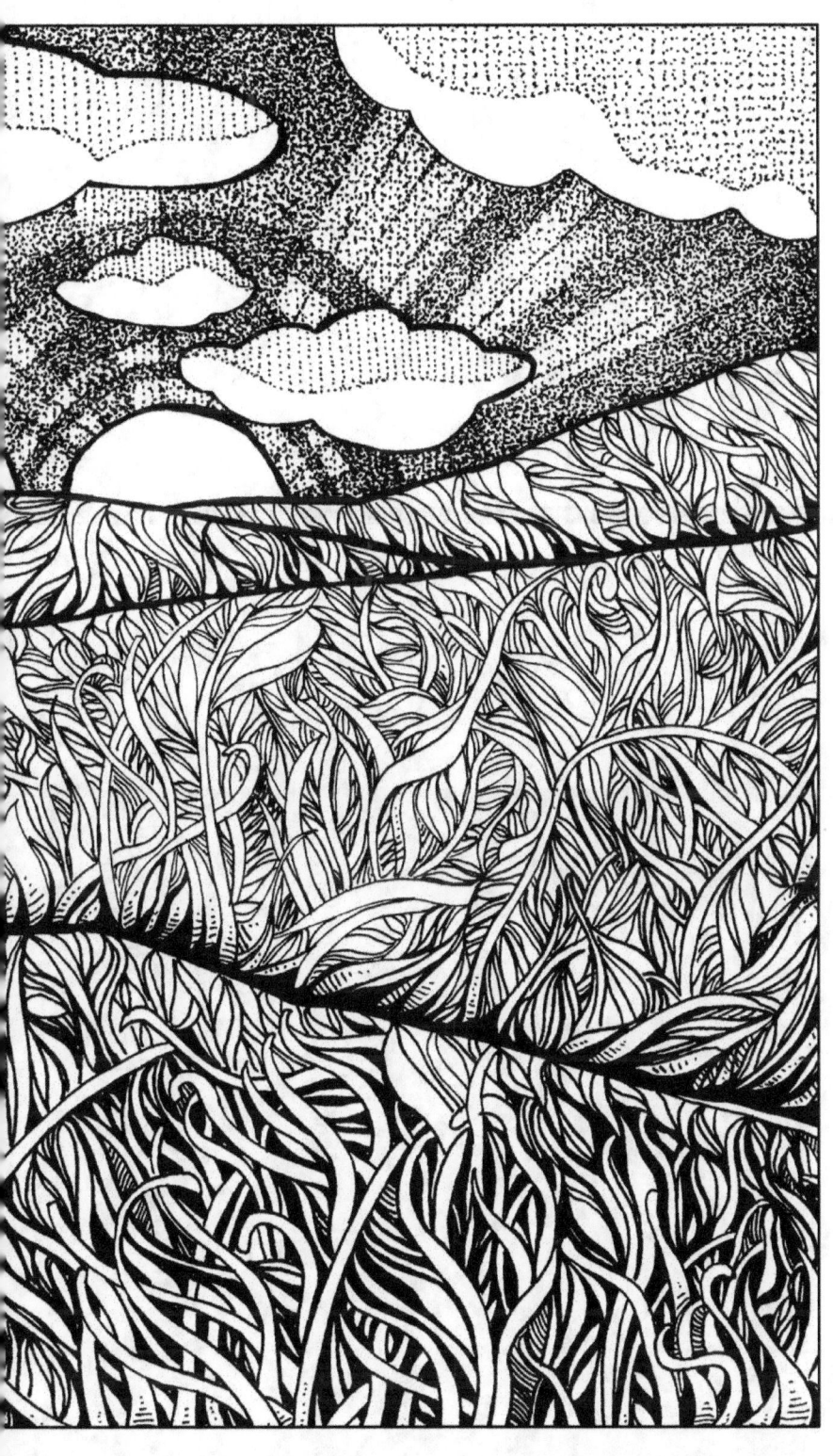

Day after day

Lightness

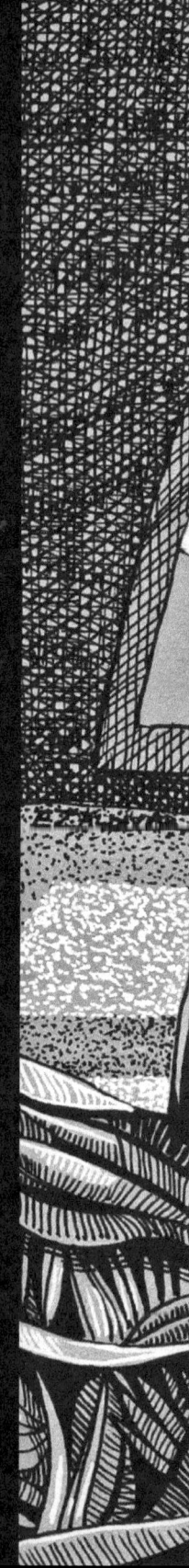

triumph of Bacchus

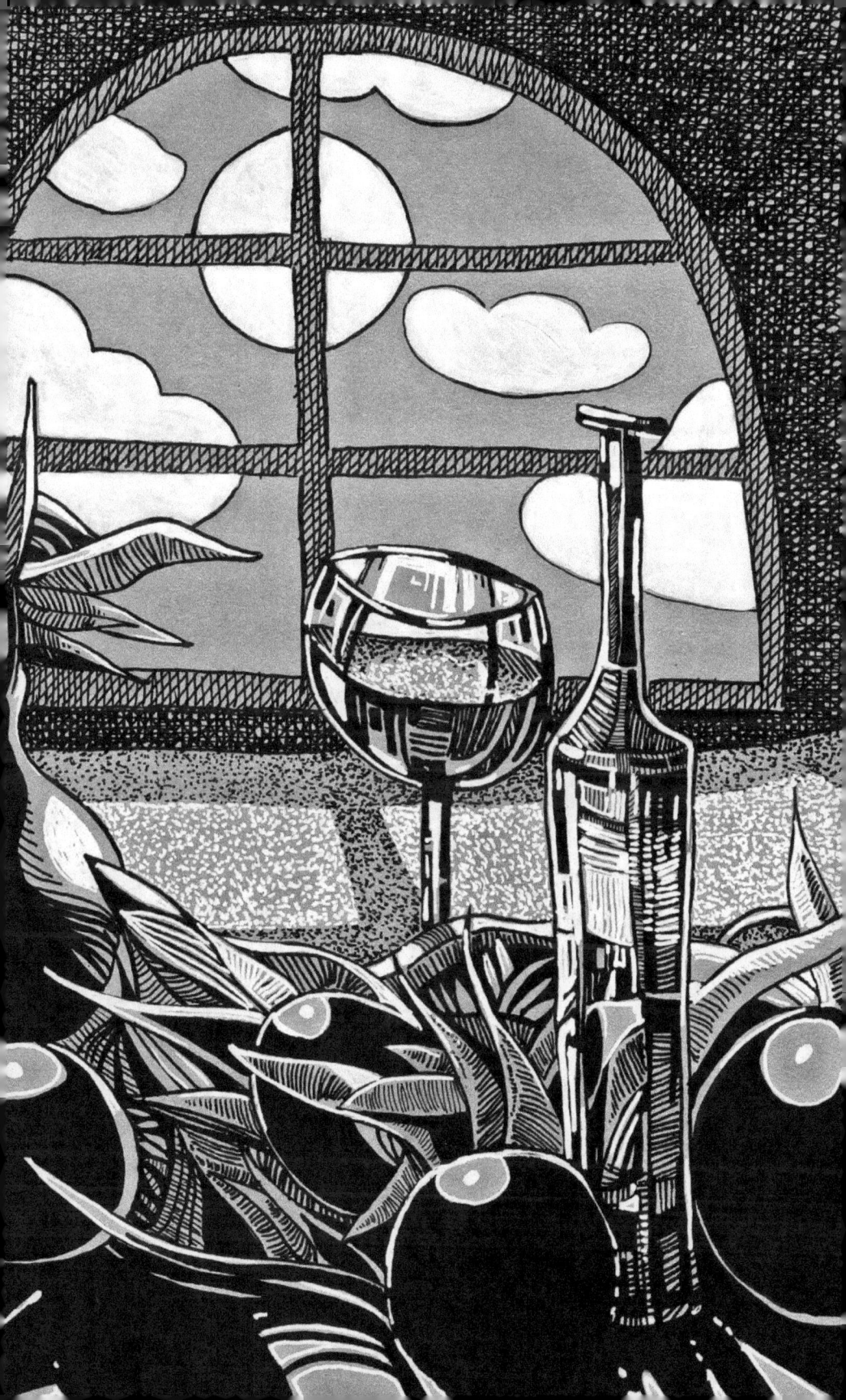

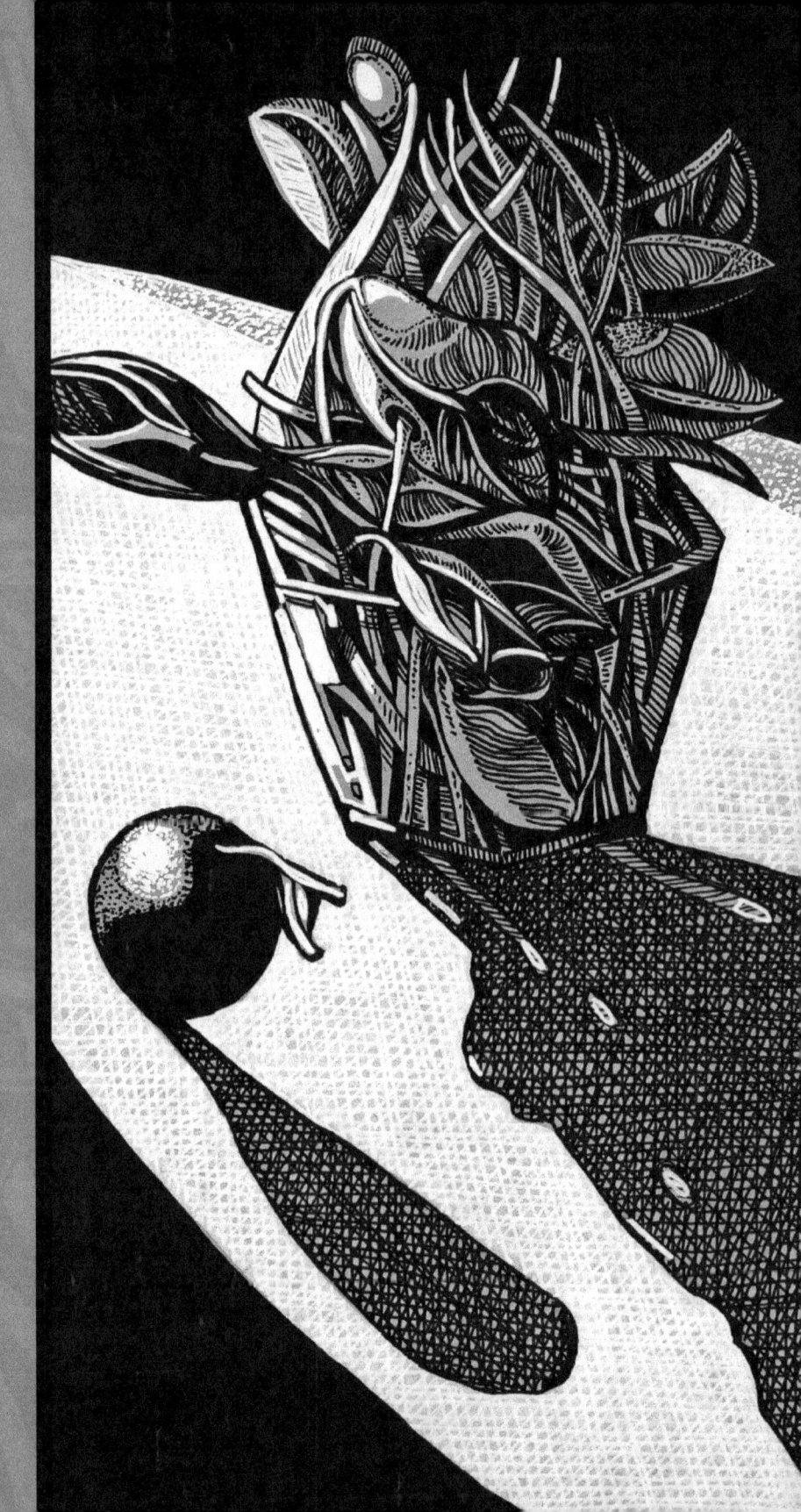

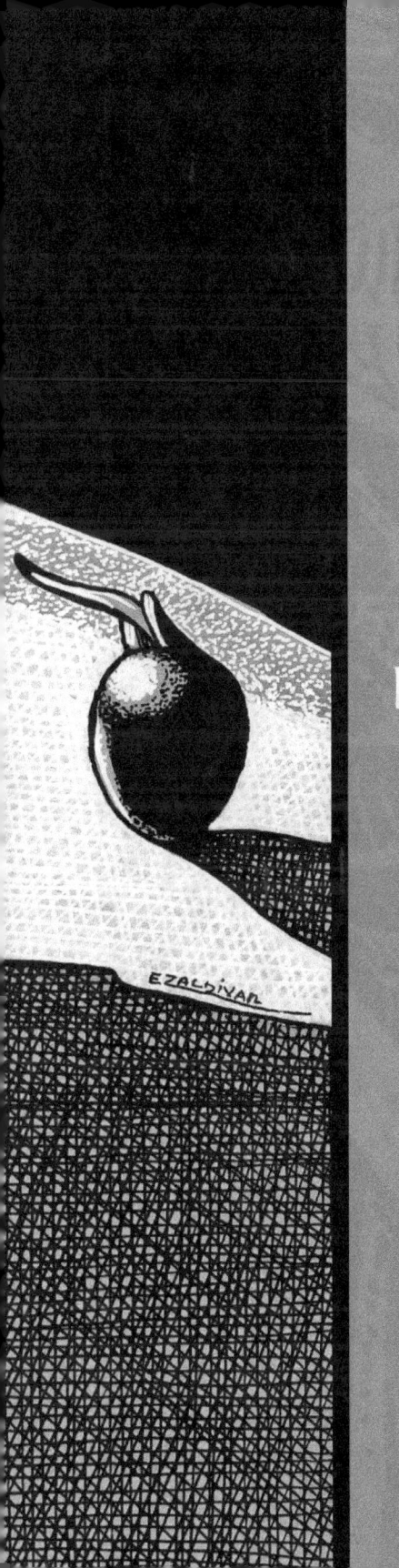

Romance of light
and shadow

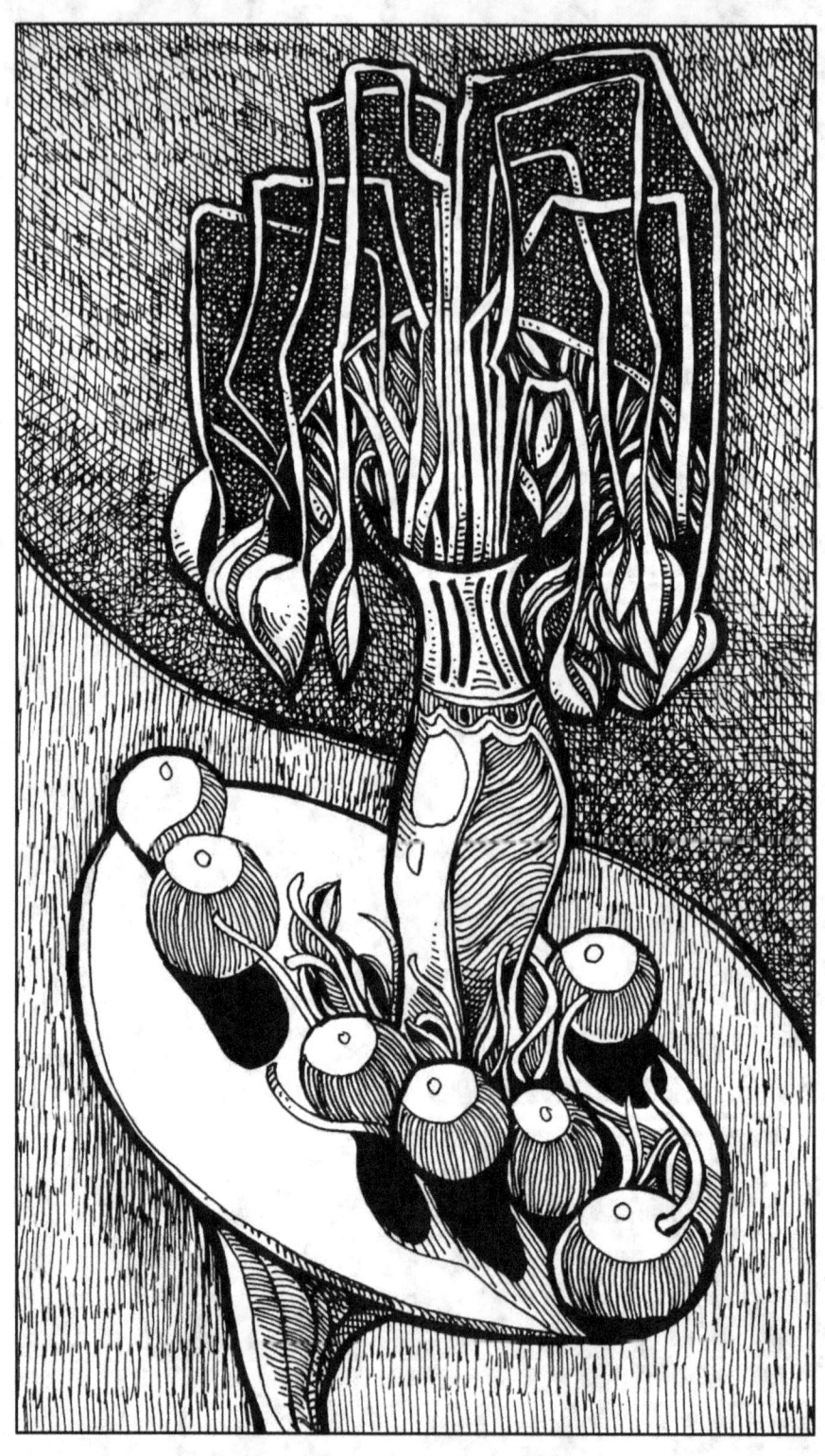

Tribute to ephemeral beauty

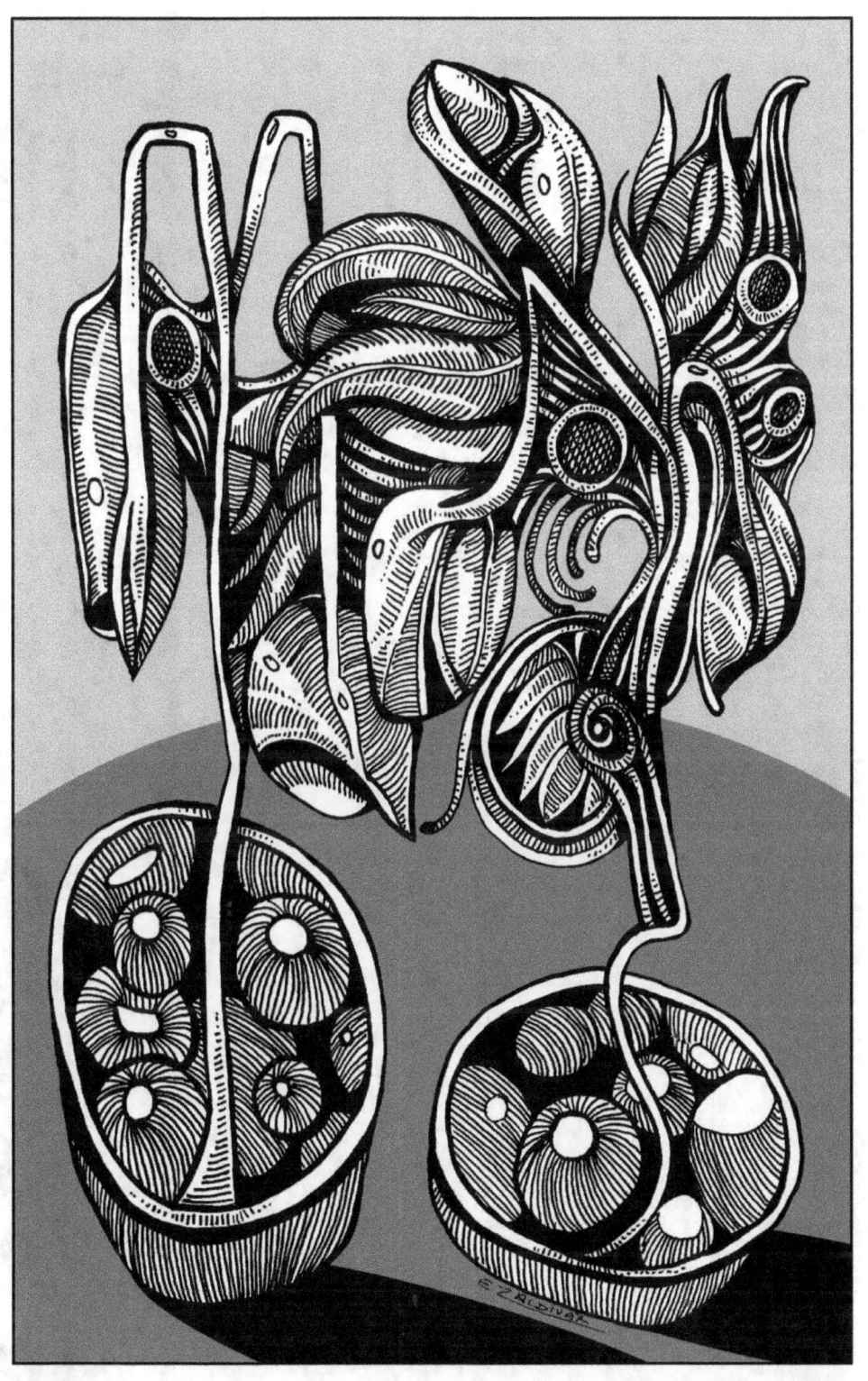

Voluptuousness

Hedonism
and contemplation

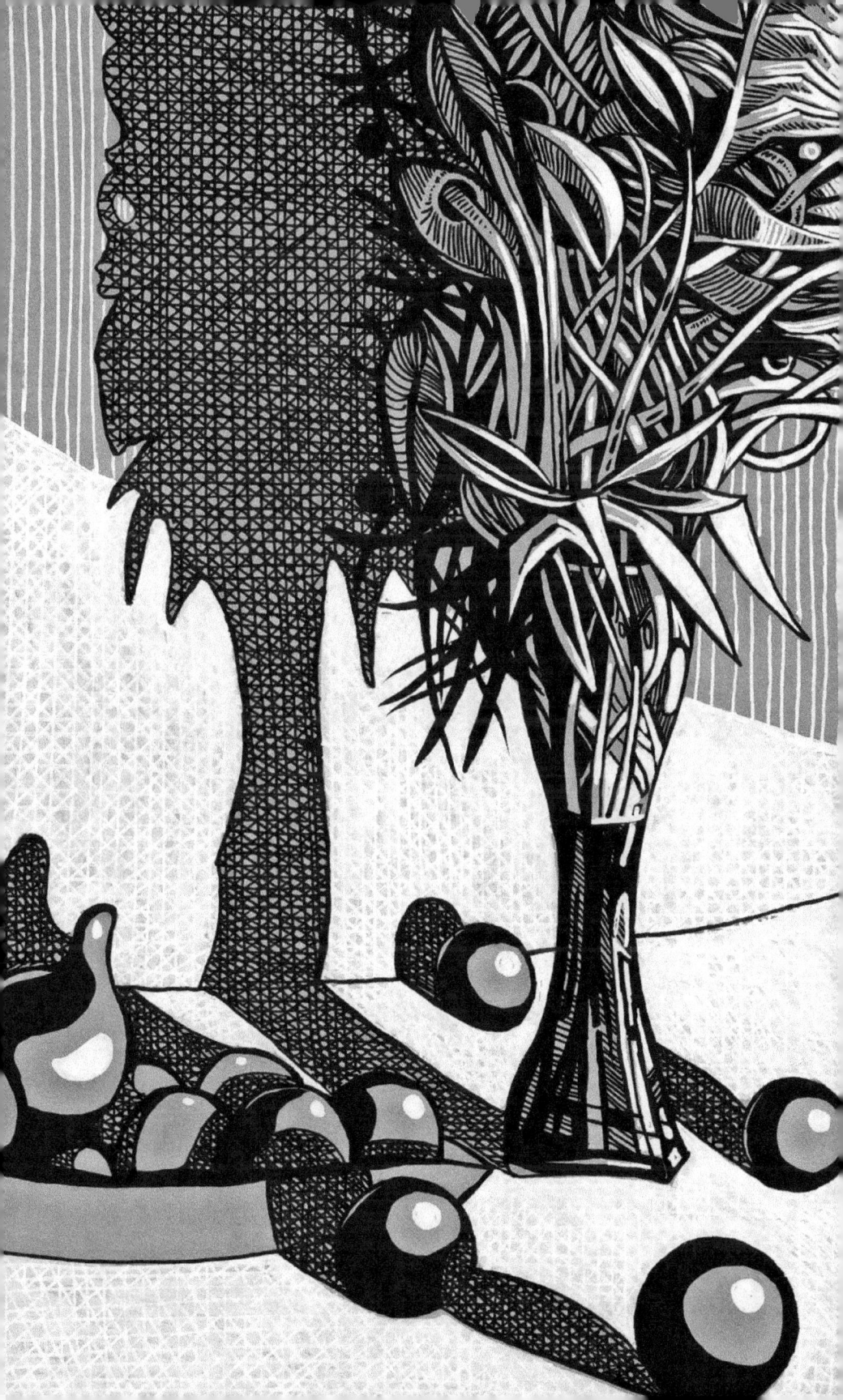

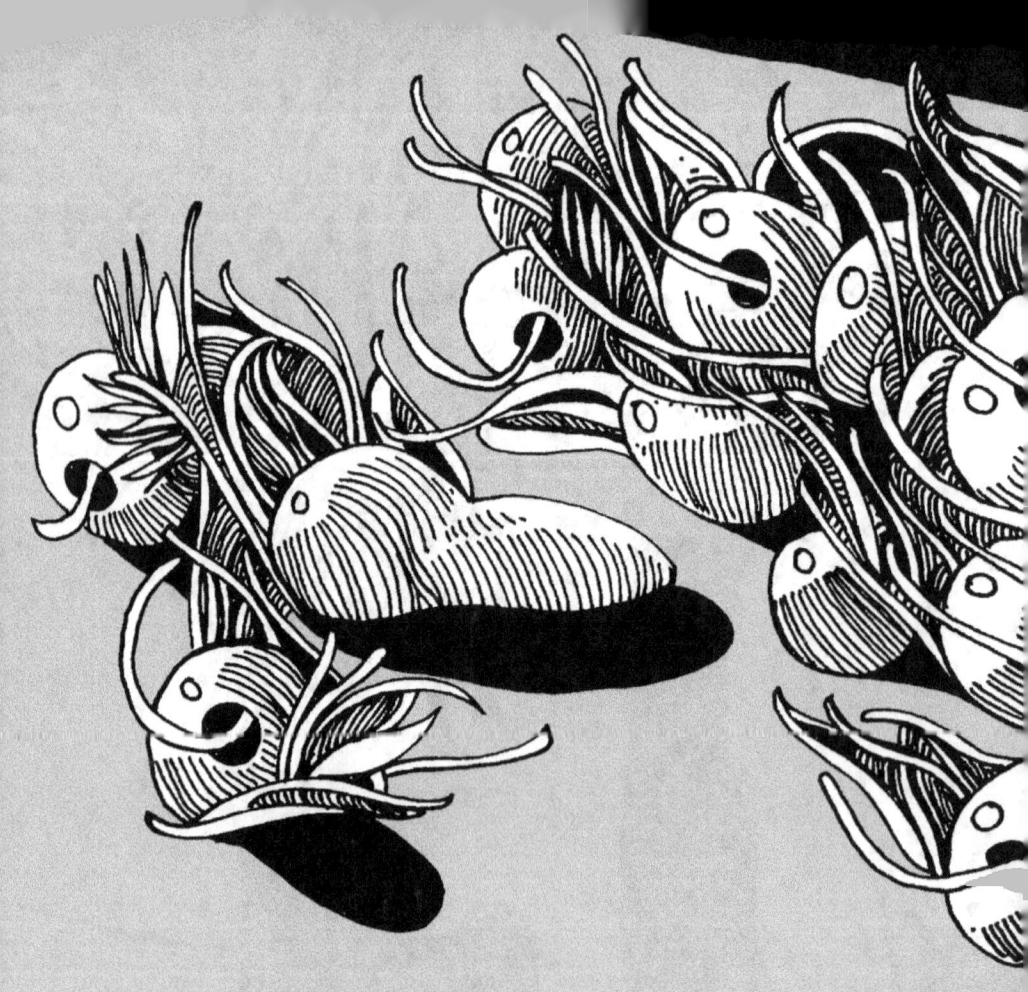

Conversations with Epicurus

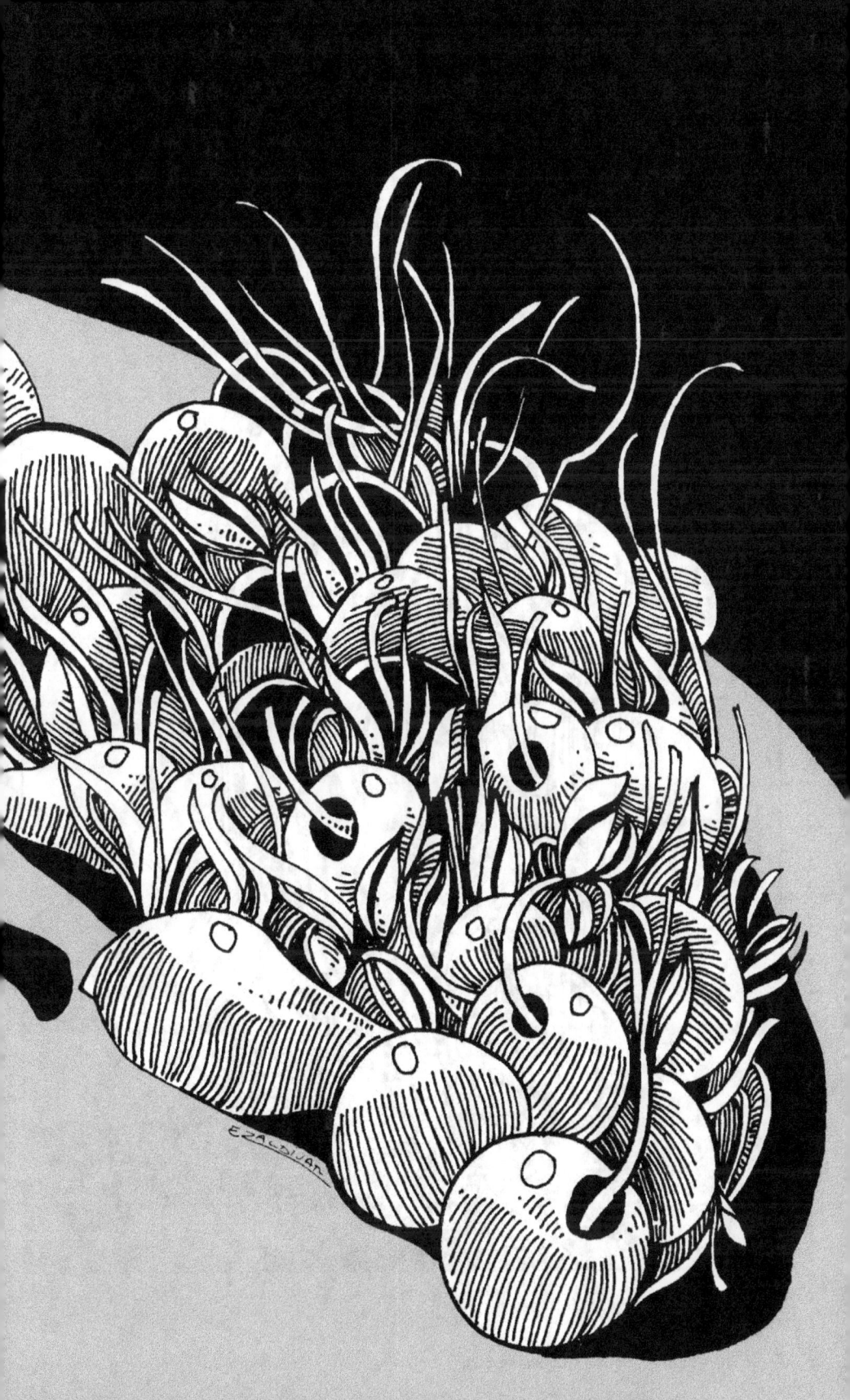

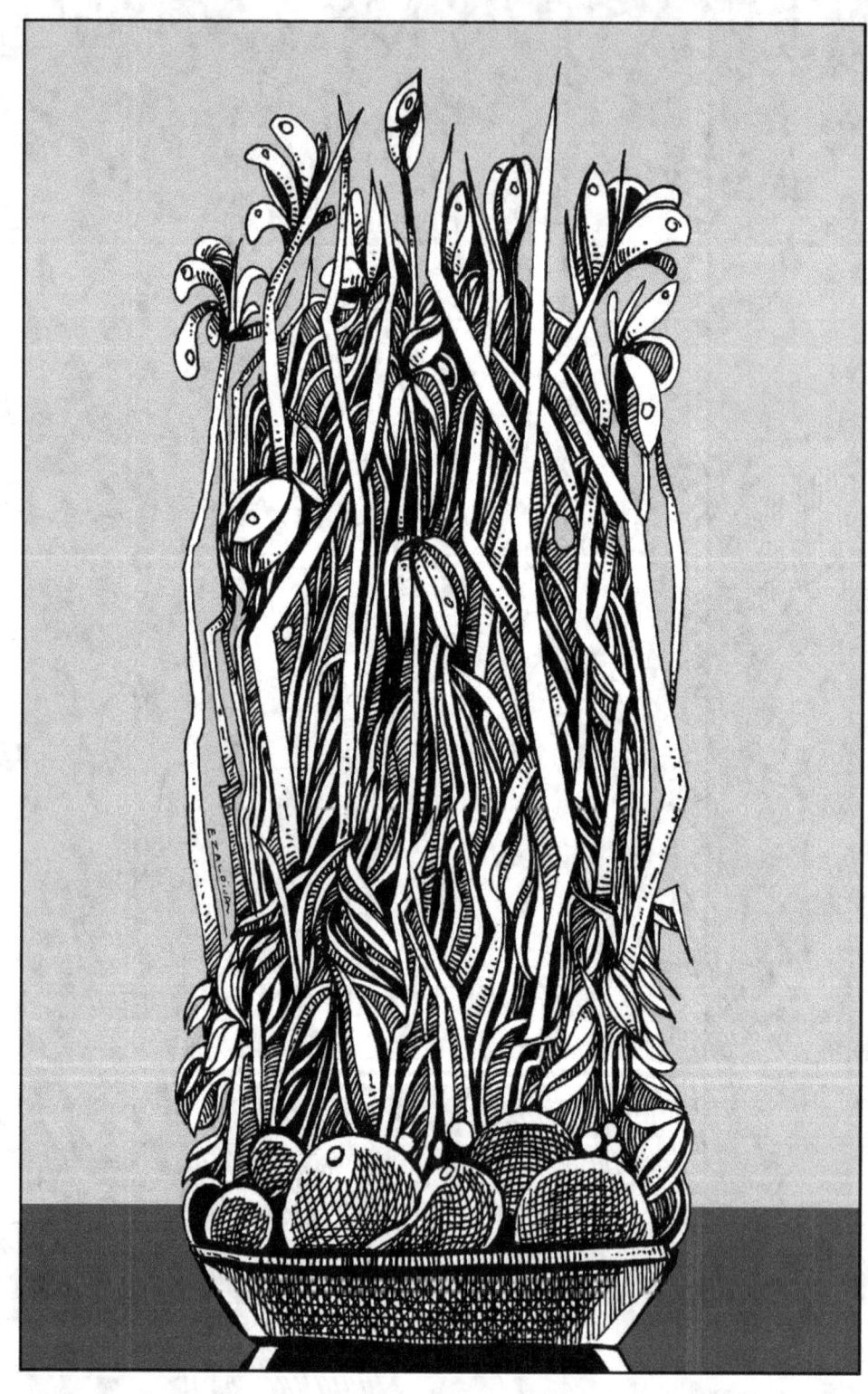

Trivial scene

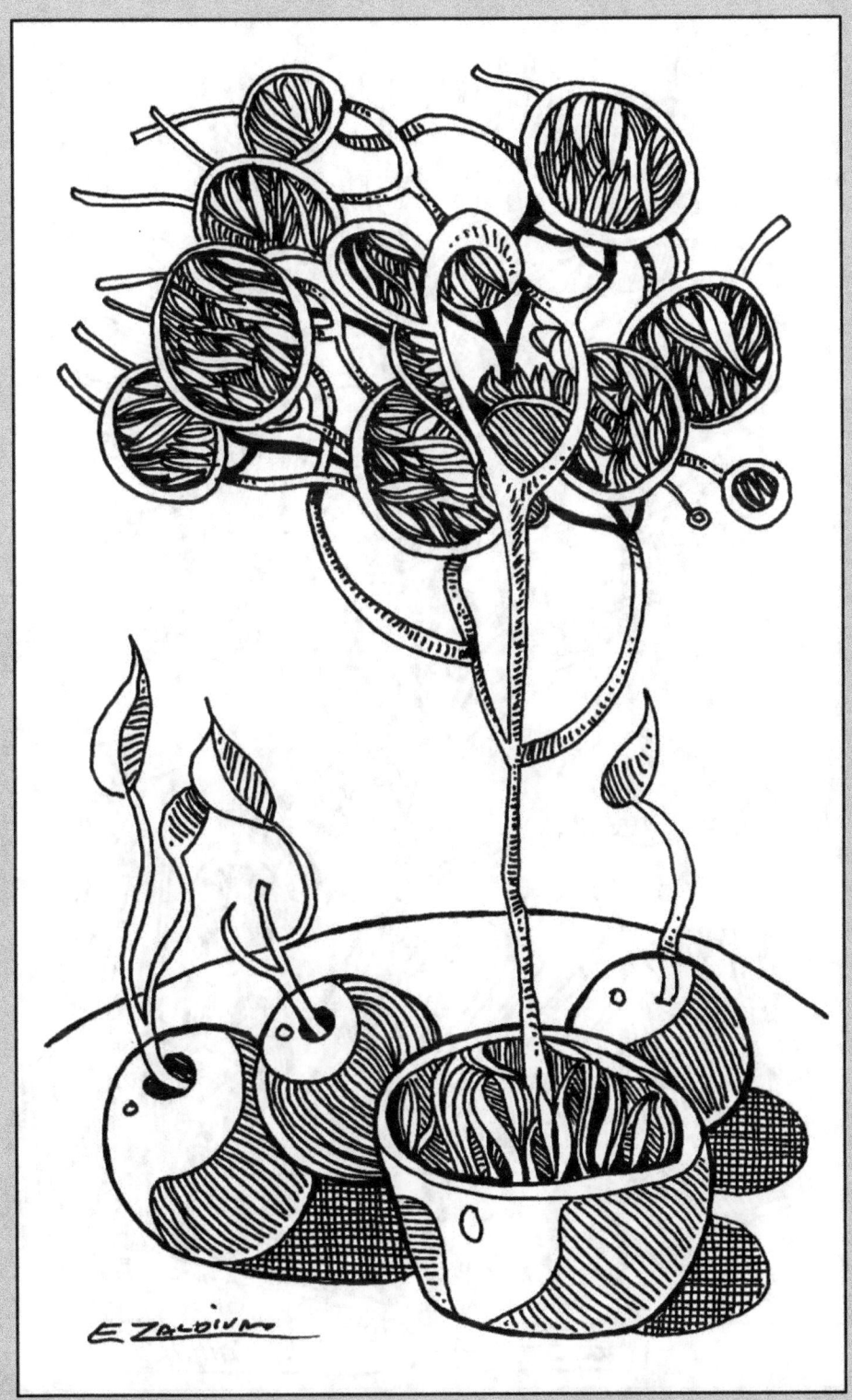

Common lives

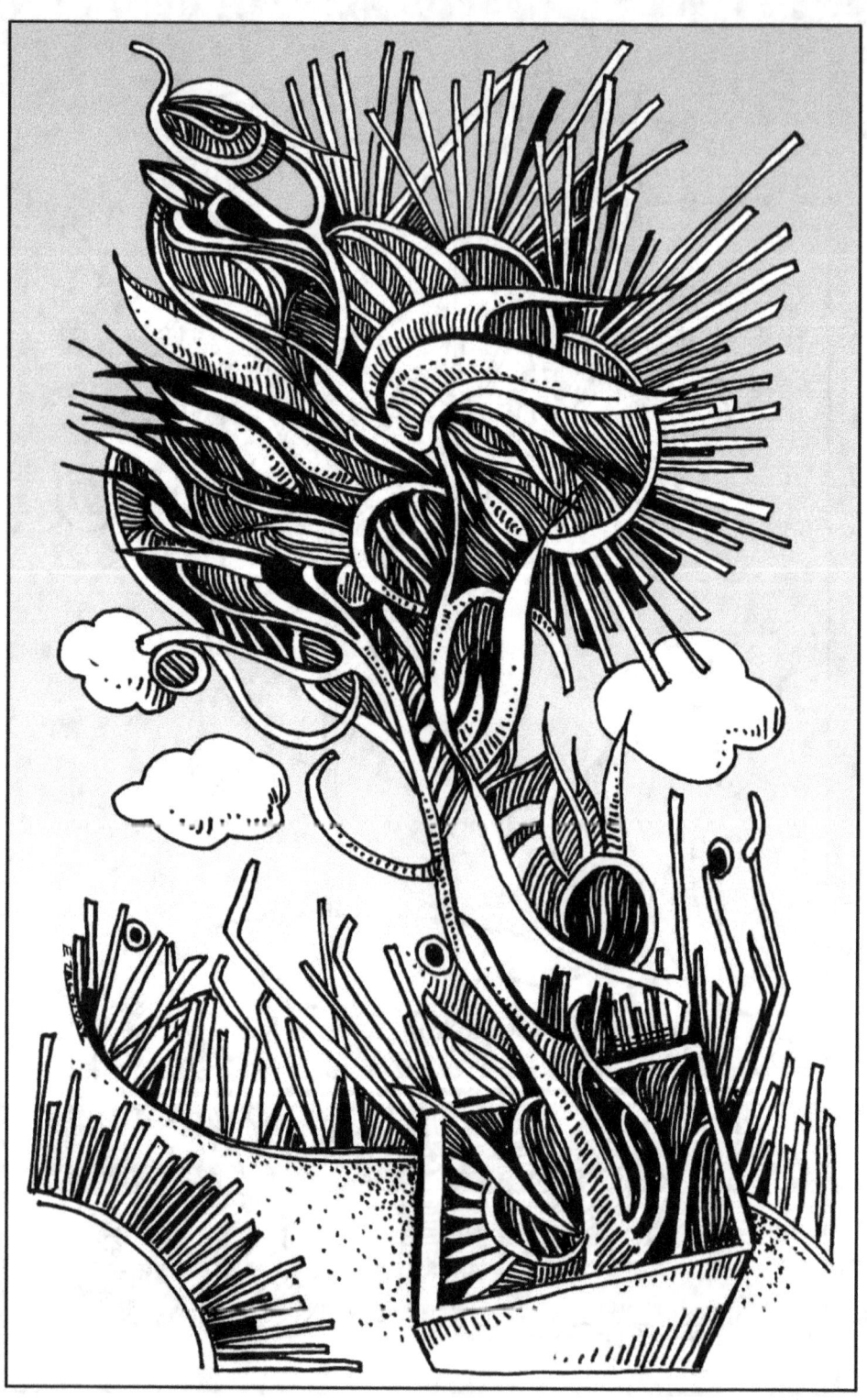

Wild flowers

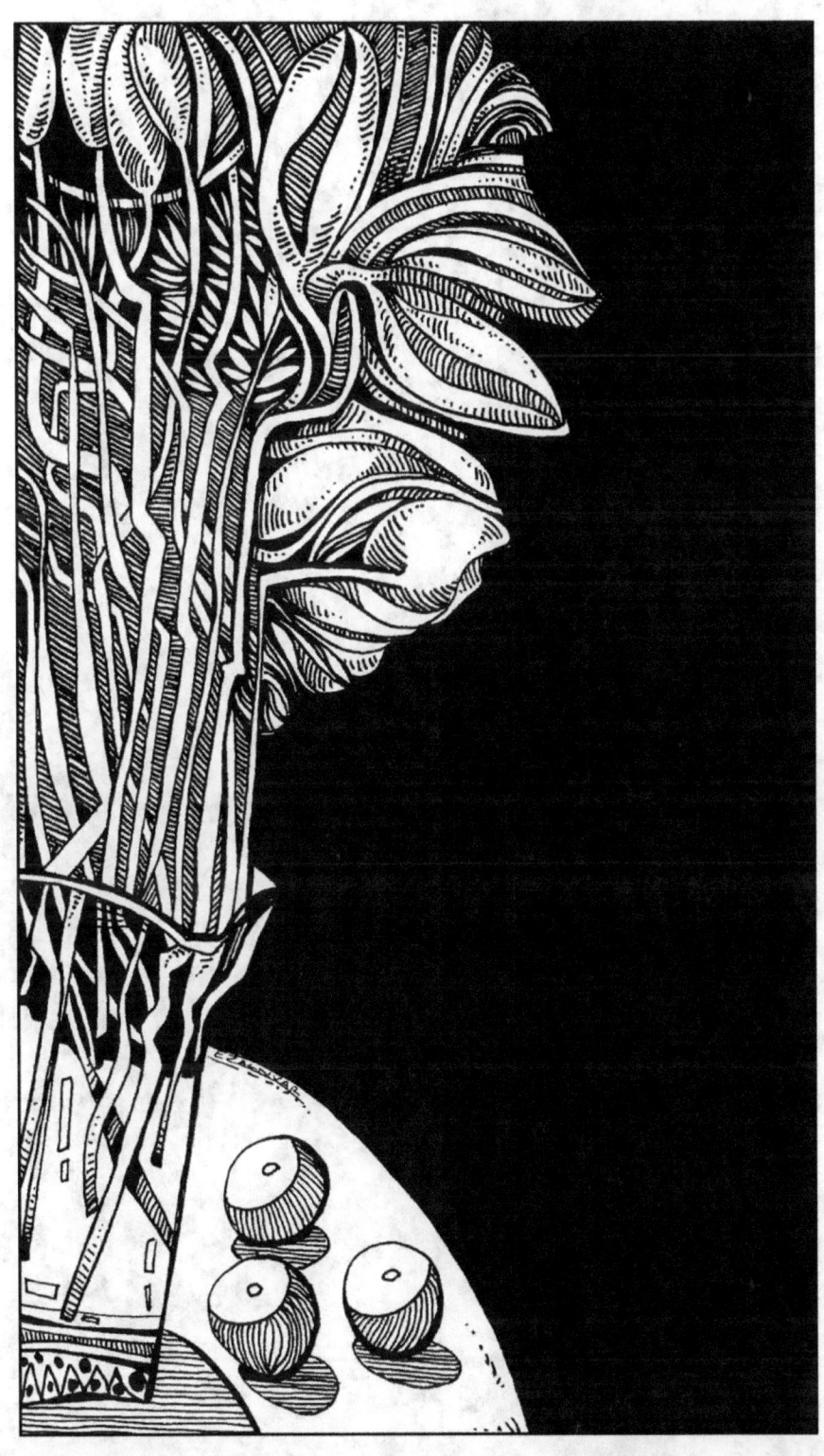

White roses

The splendor of a brief
moment in the window

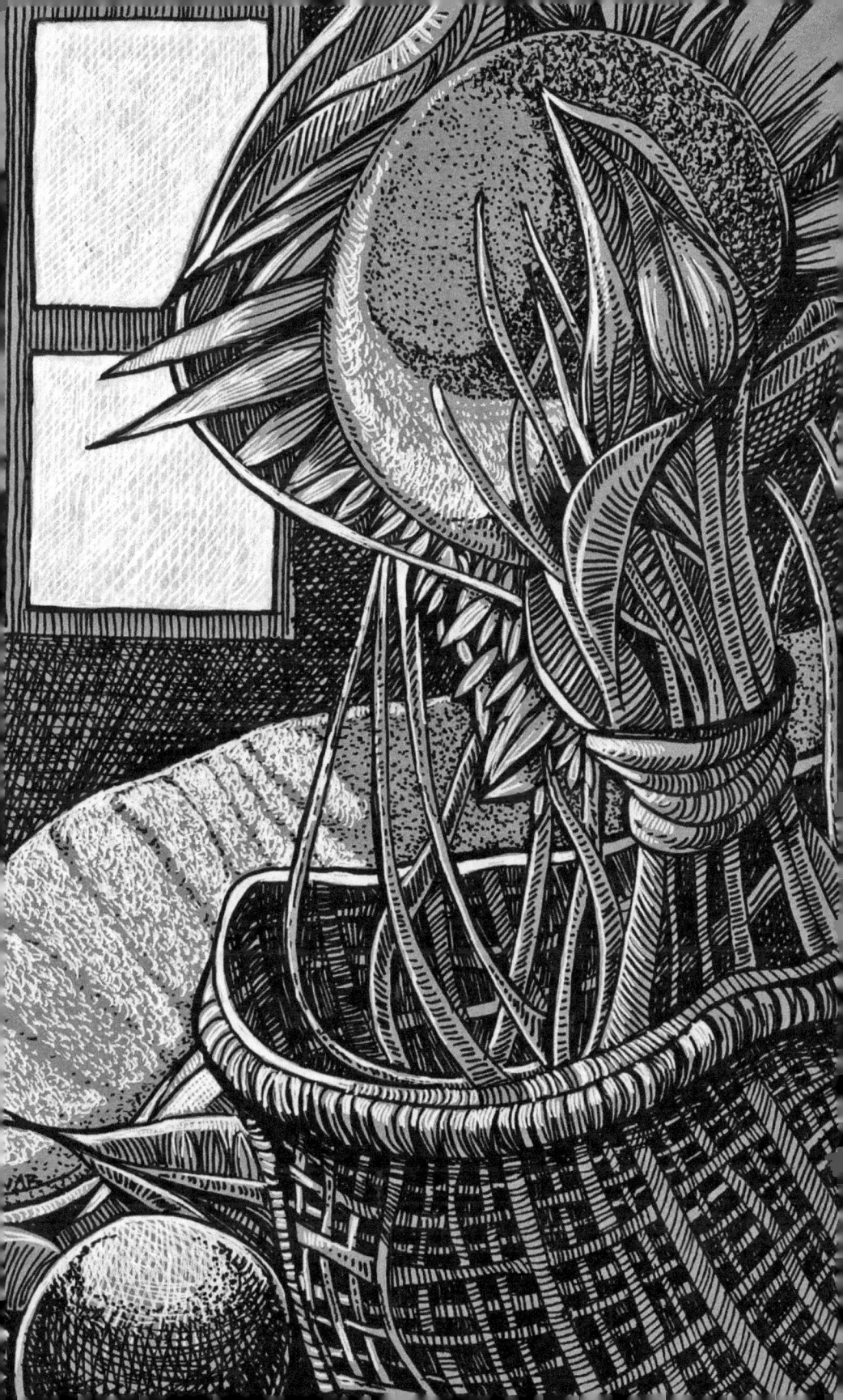

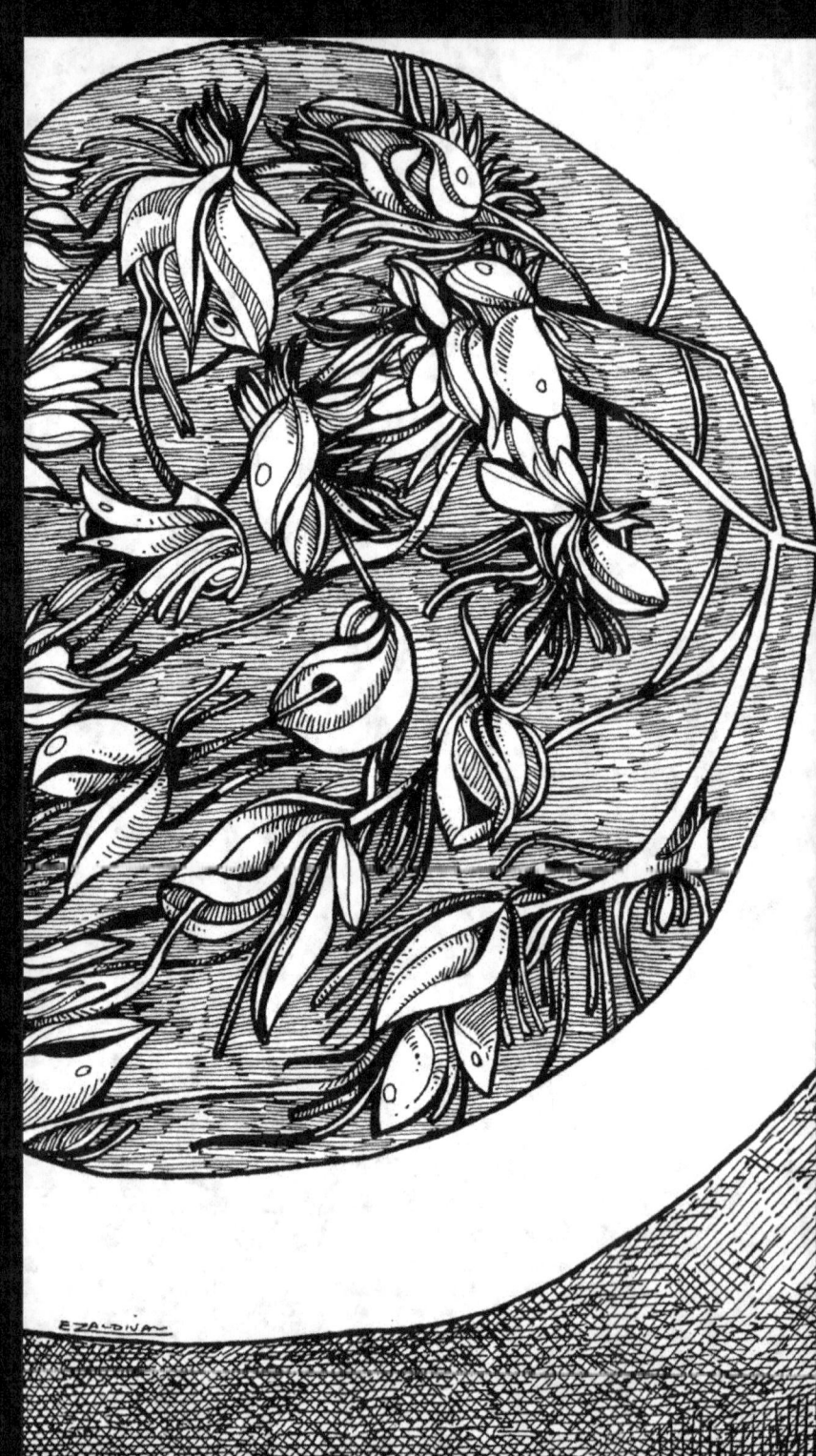

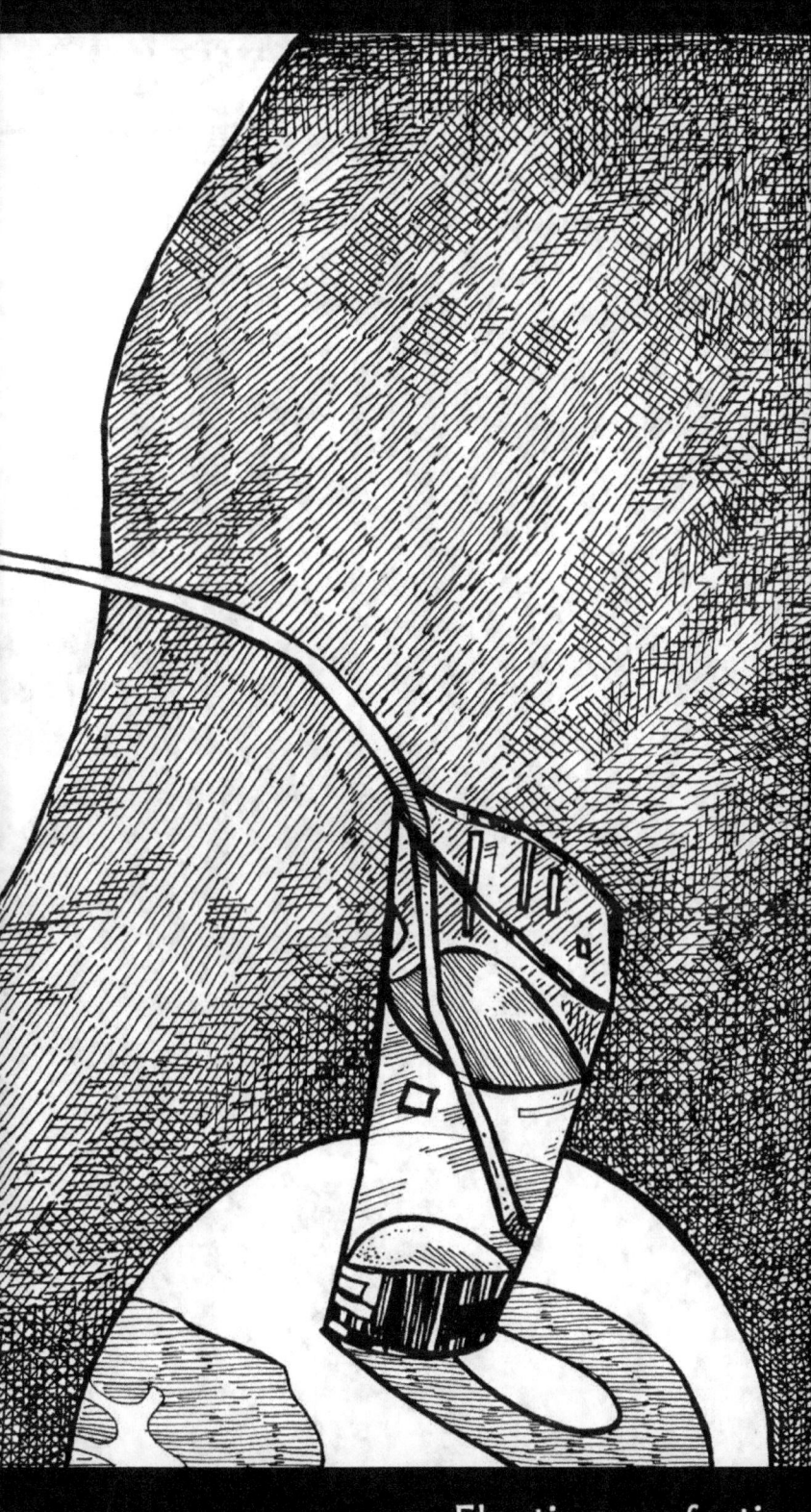

Fleeting perfection

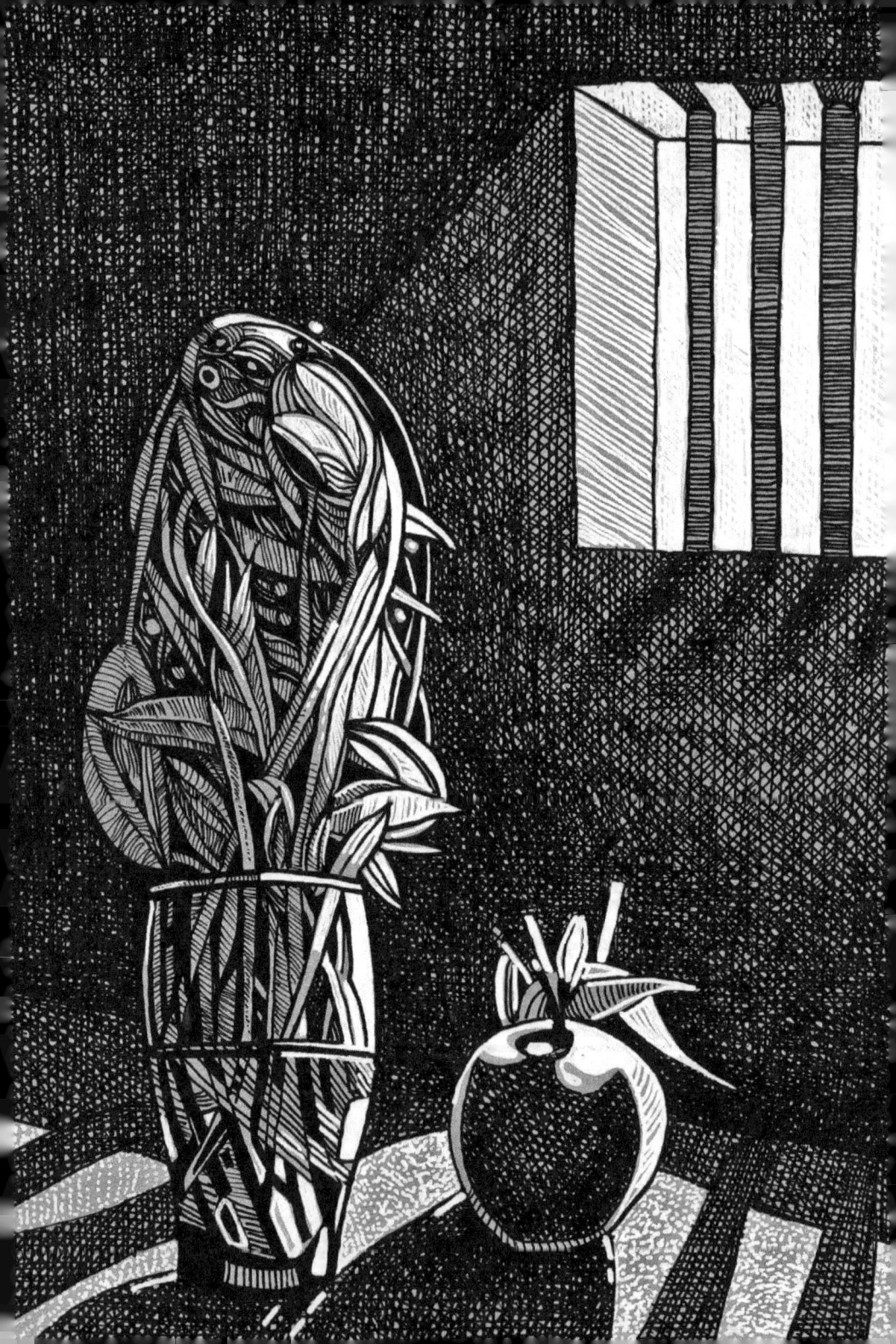

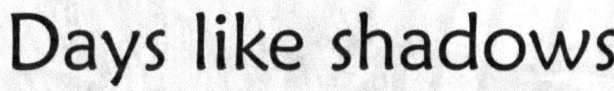

Days like shadows

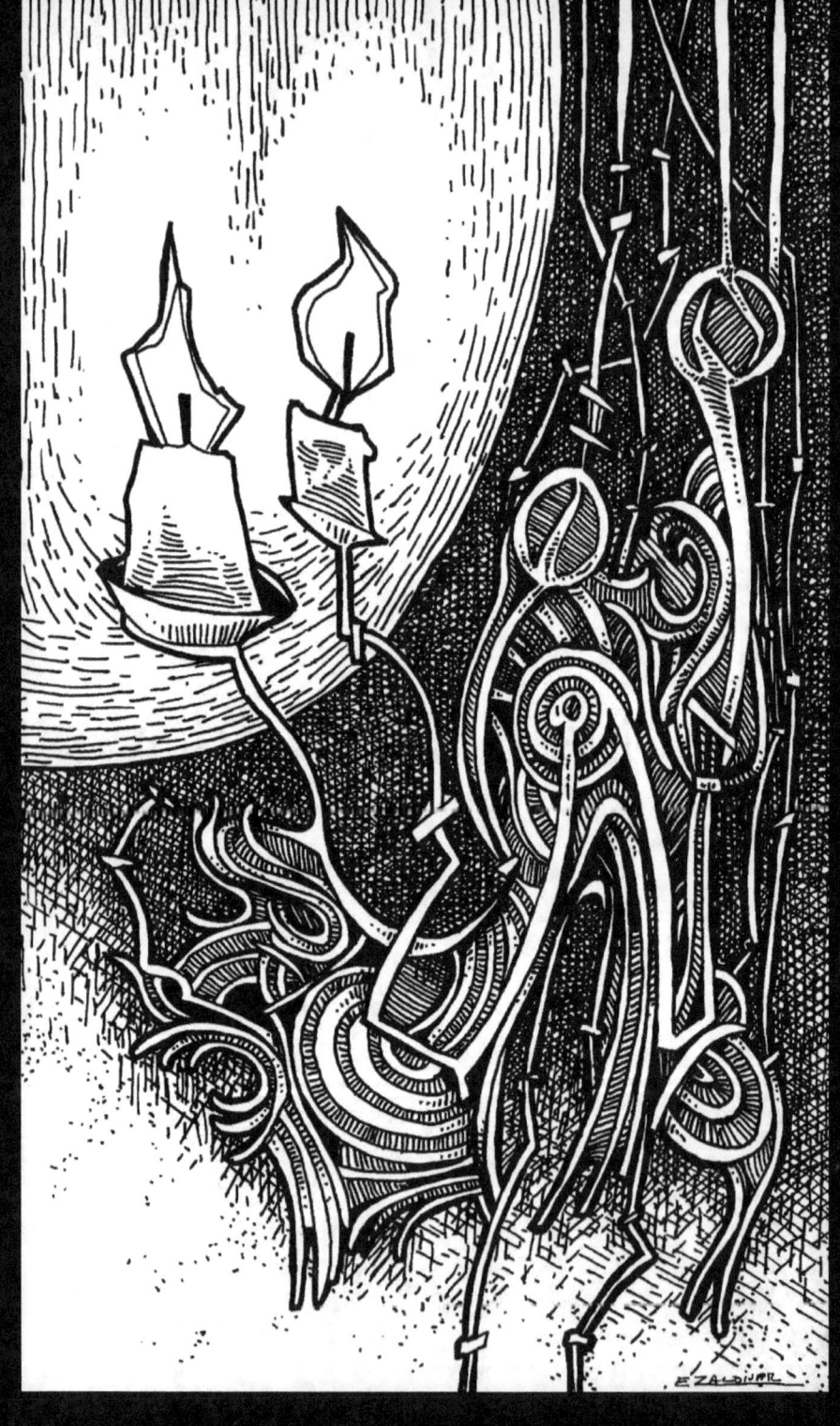

Tearing the gloom

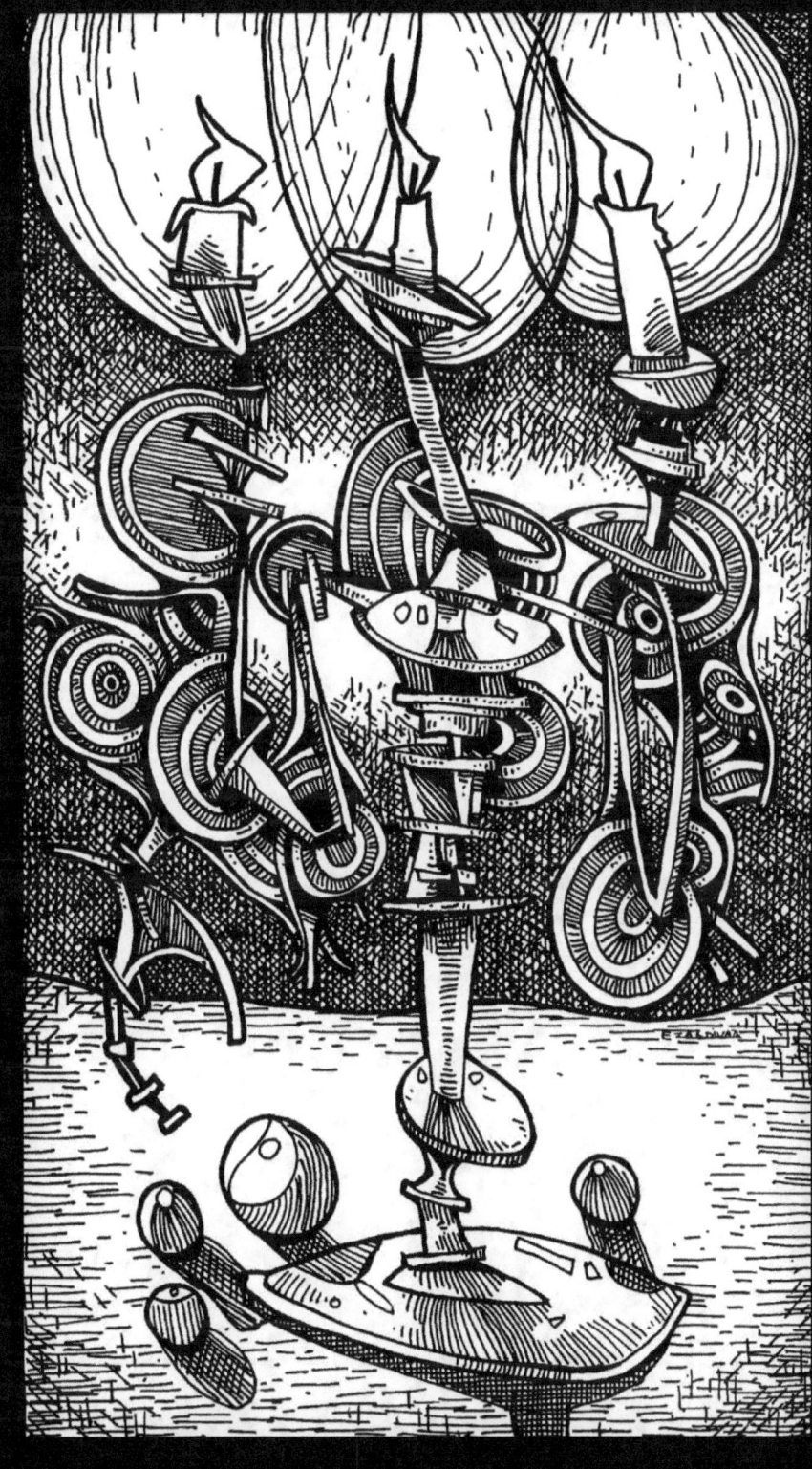

While the light lasts

Facades

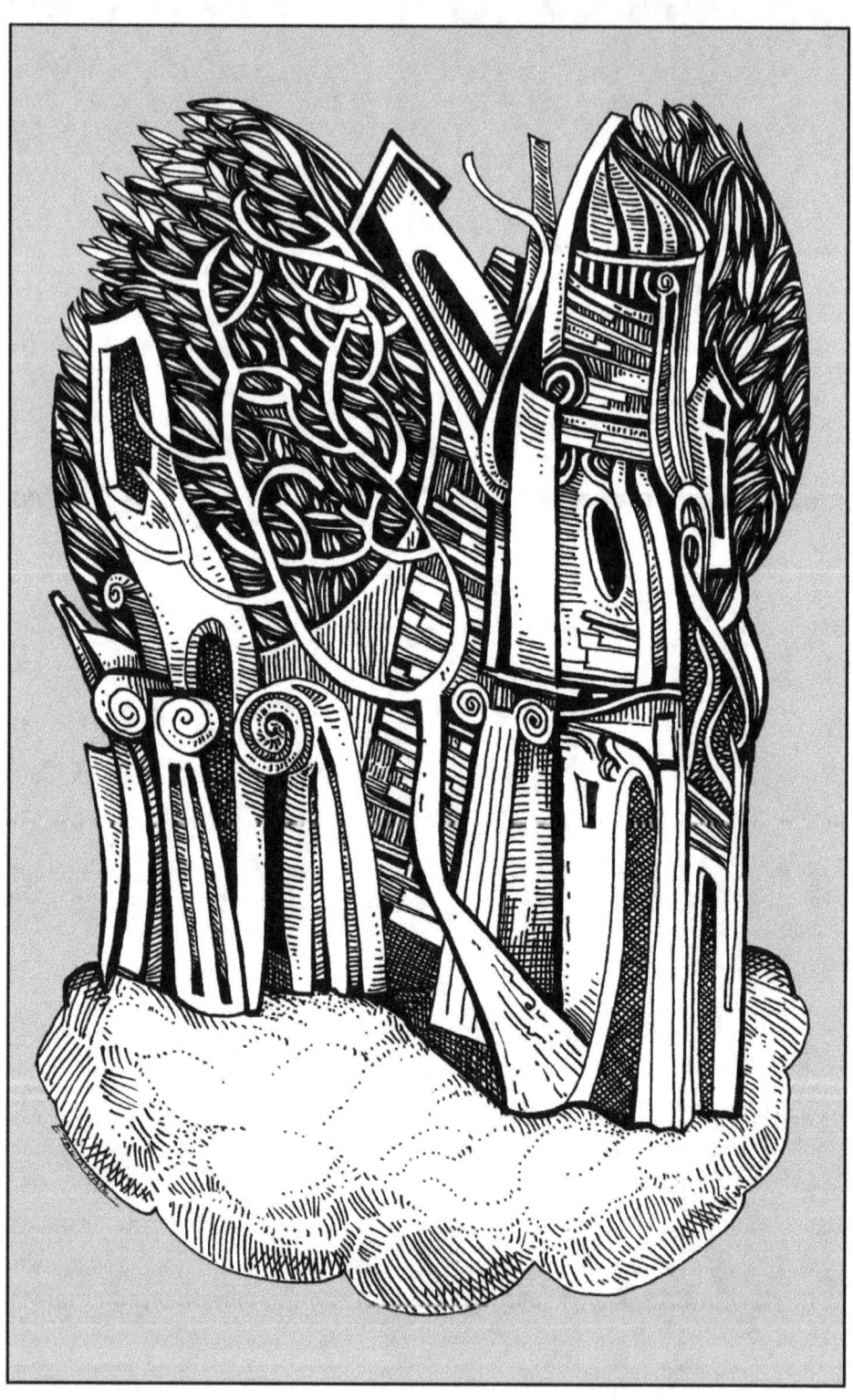

Floating island

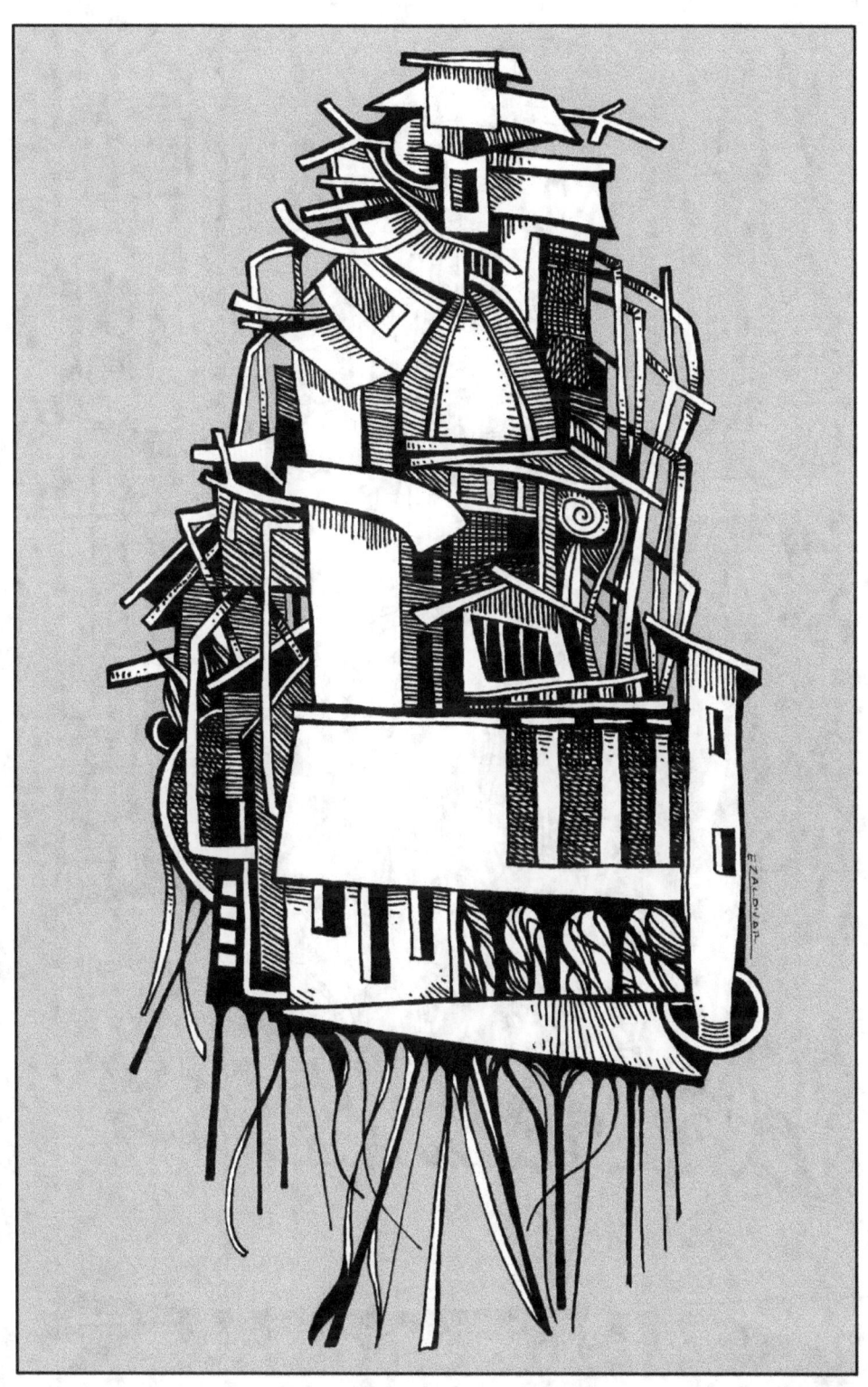

Lost city

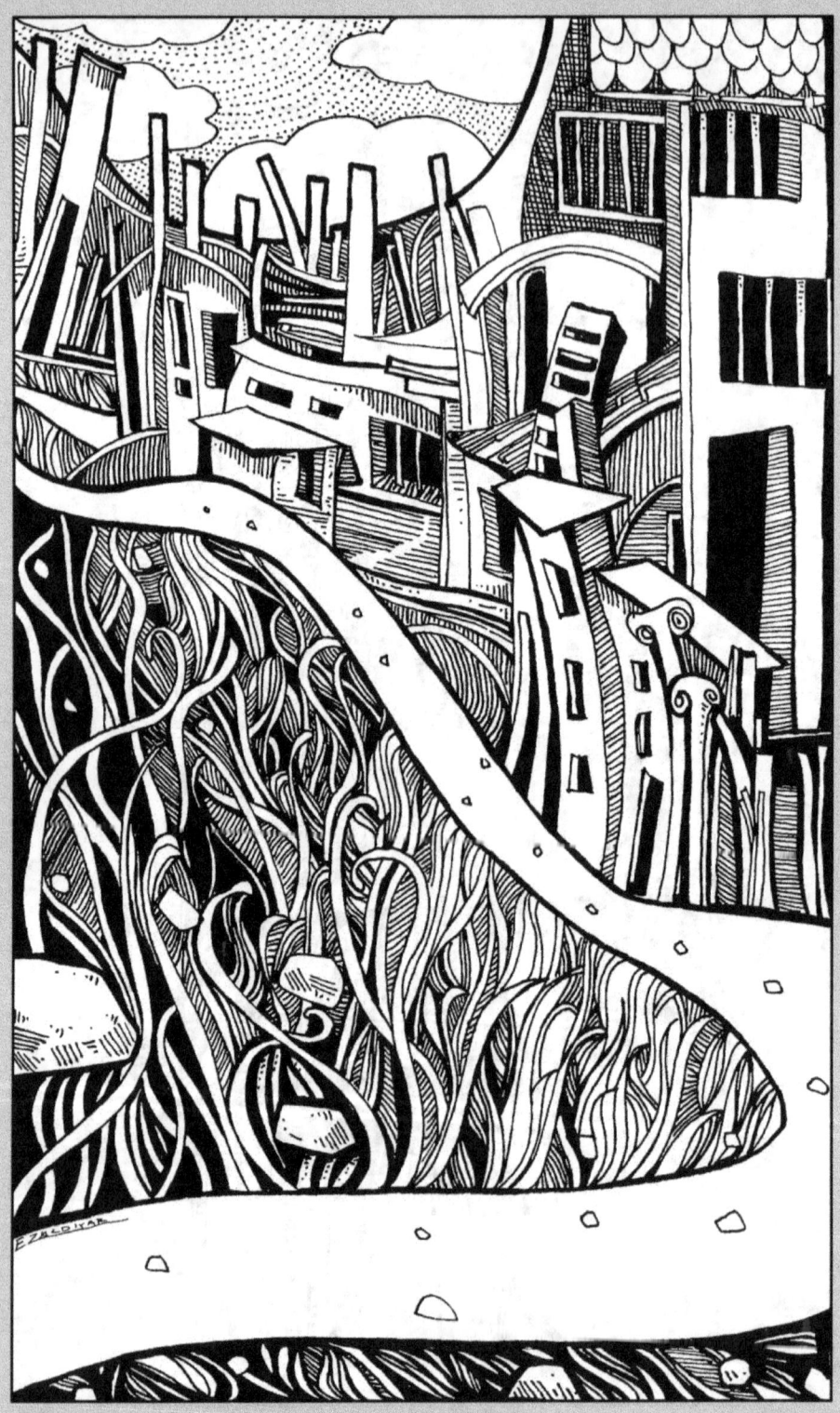

The lonely city

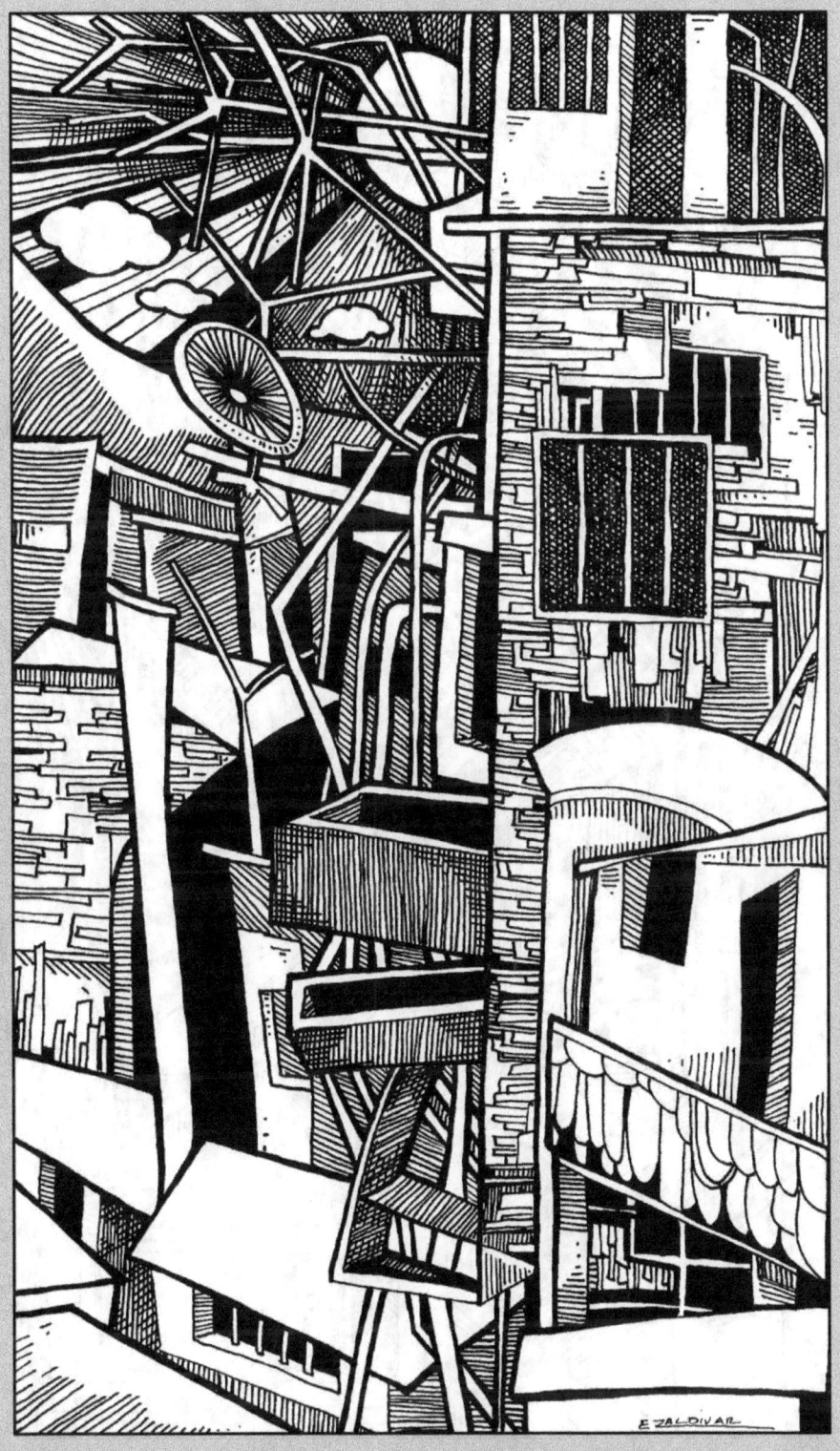

Slum

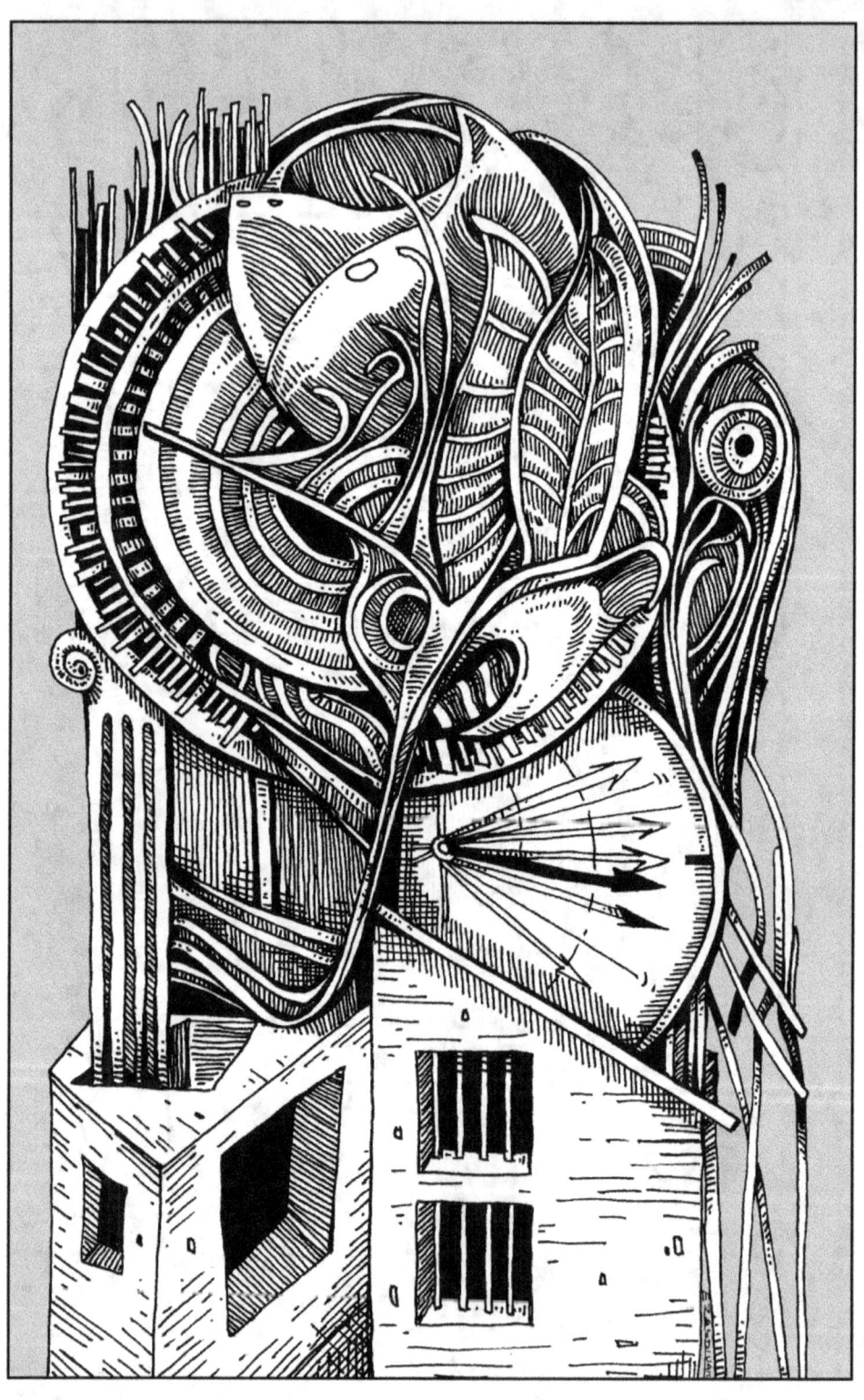

Cathedral

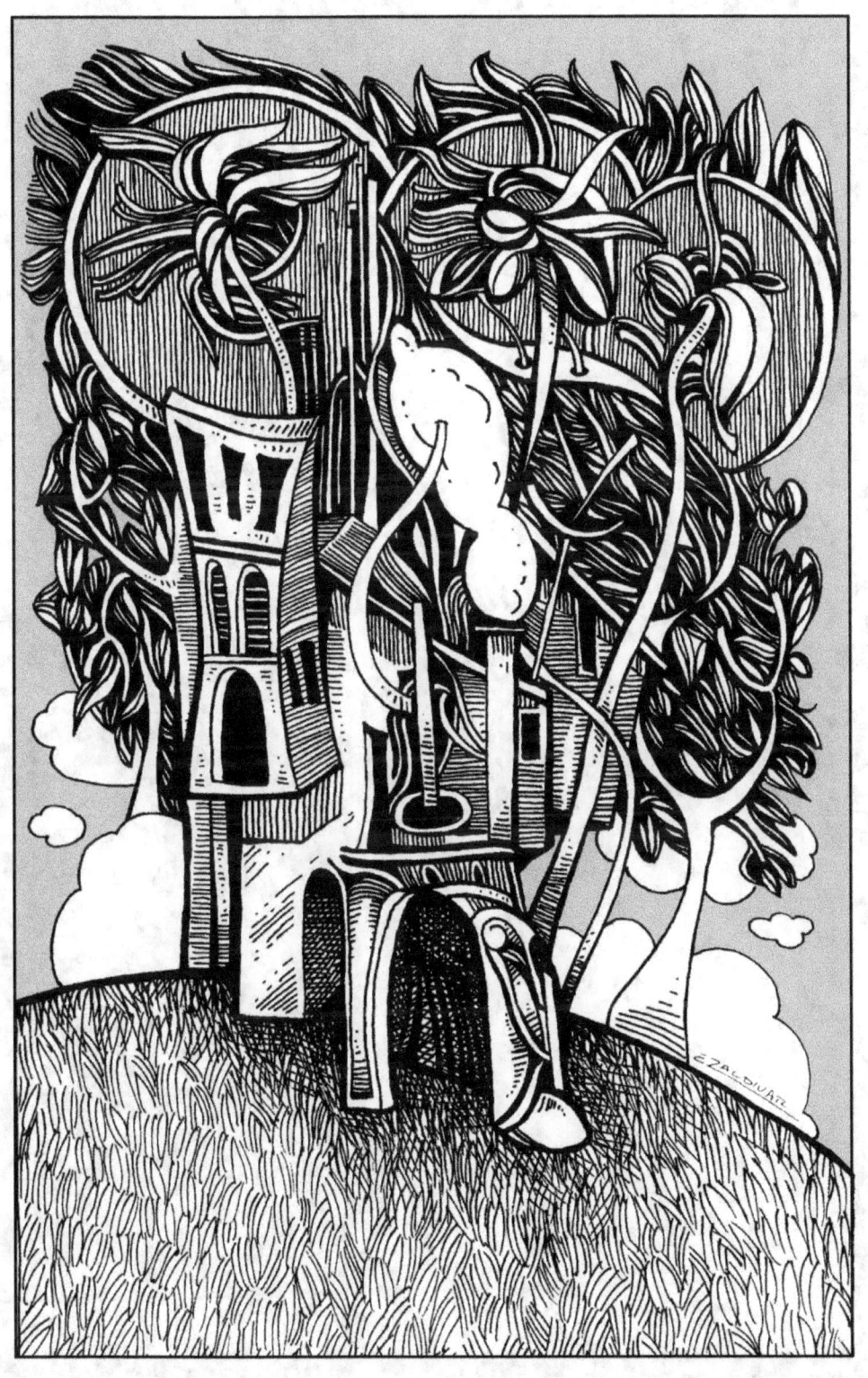

Cottage

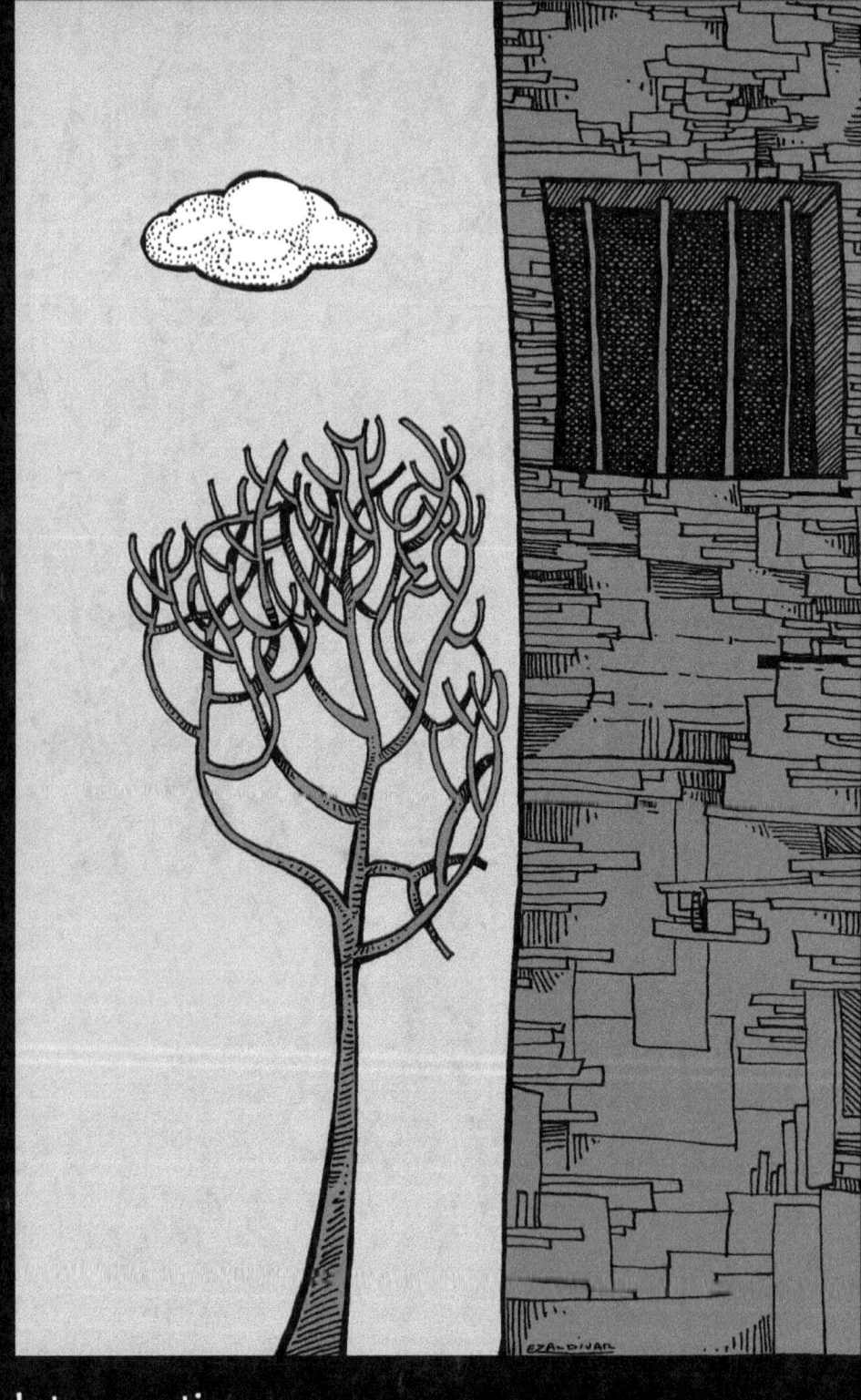

Introspection

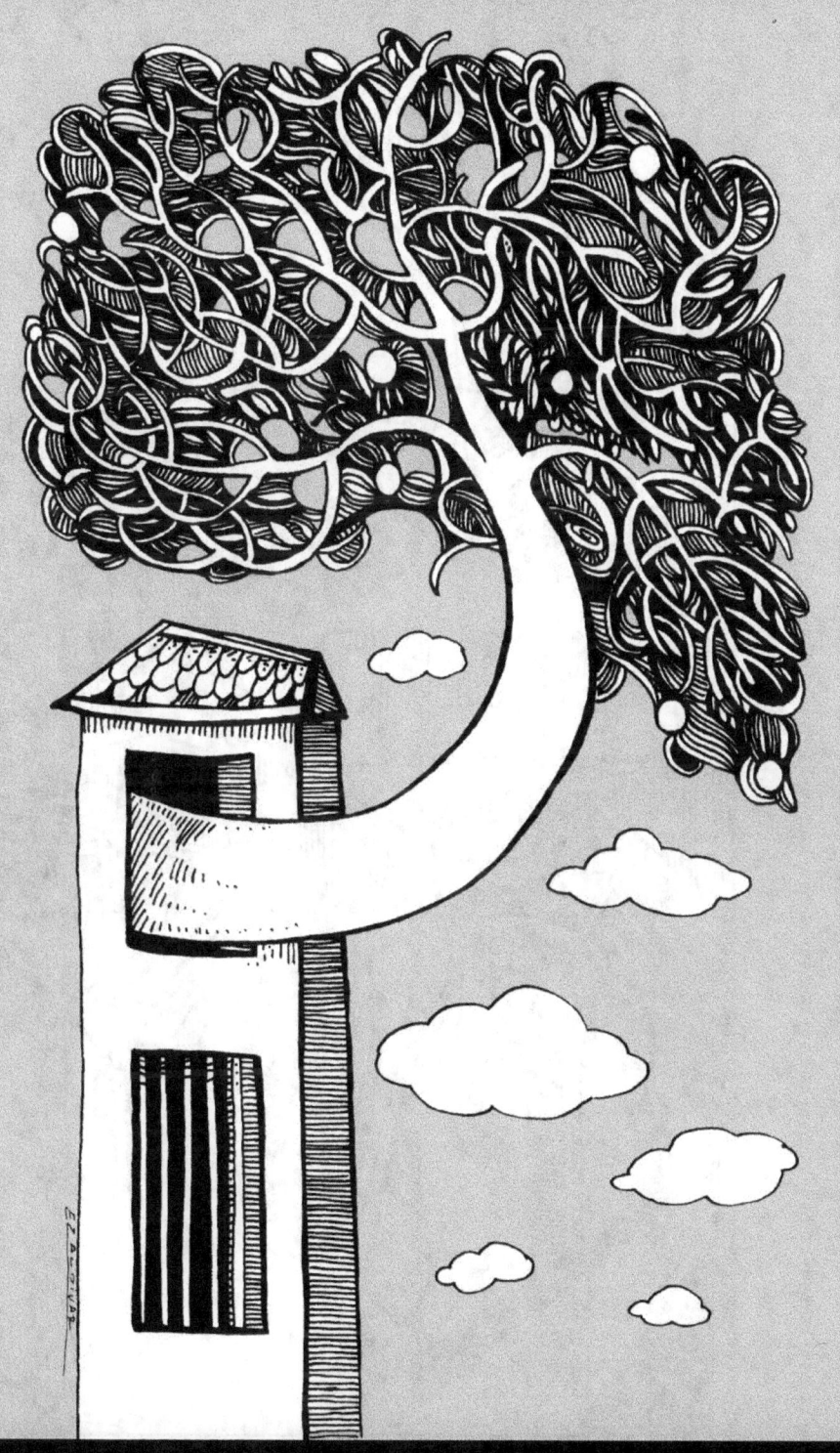

Inner world

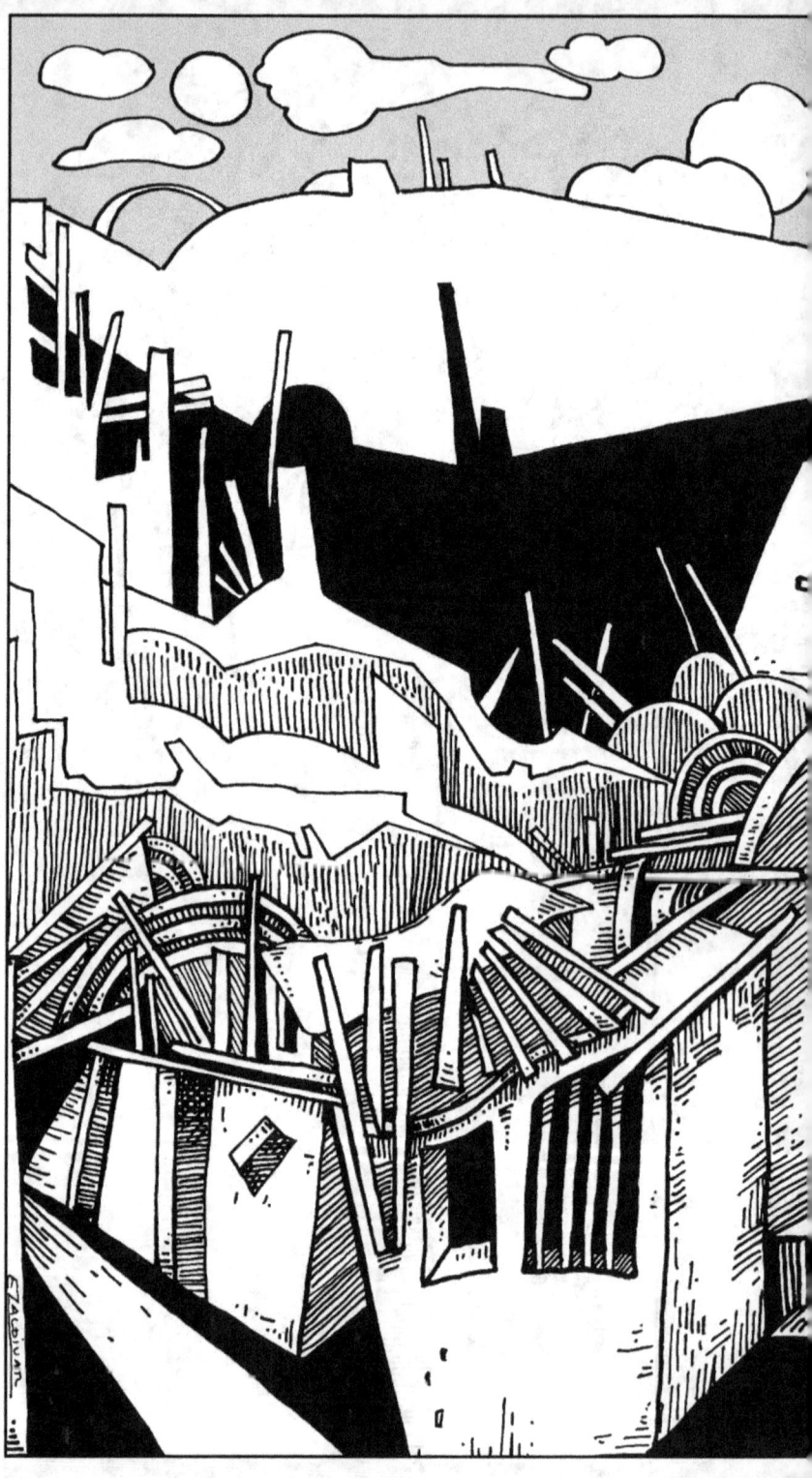

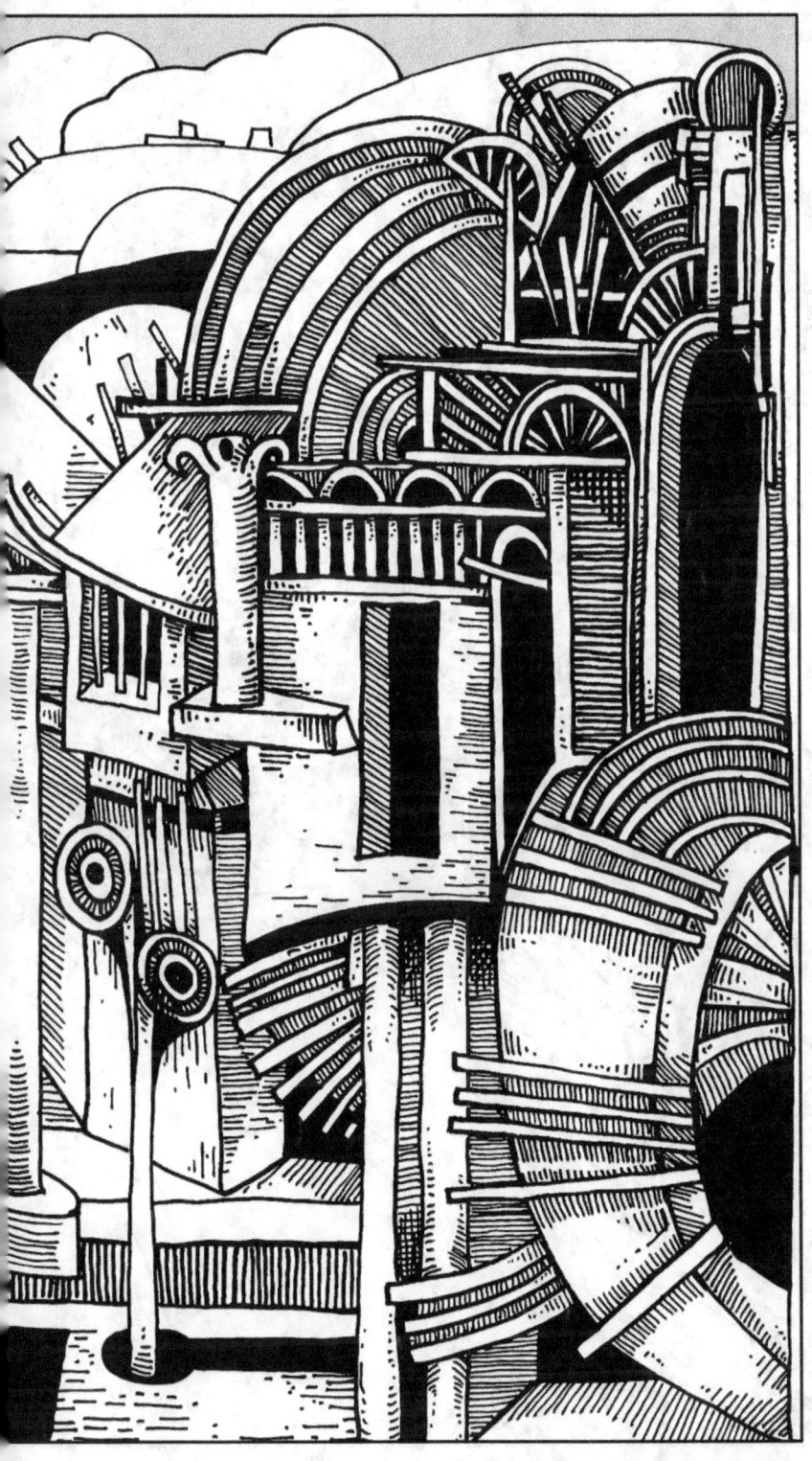

Labyrinth

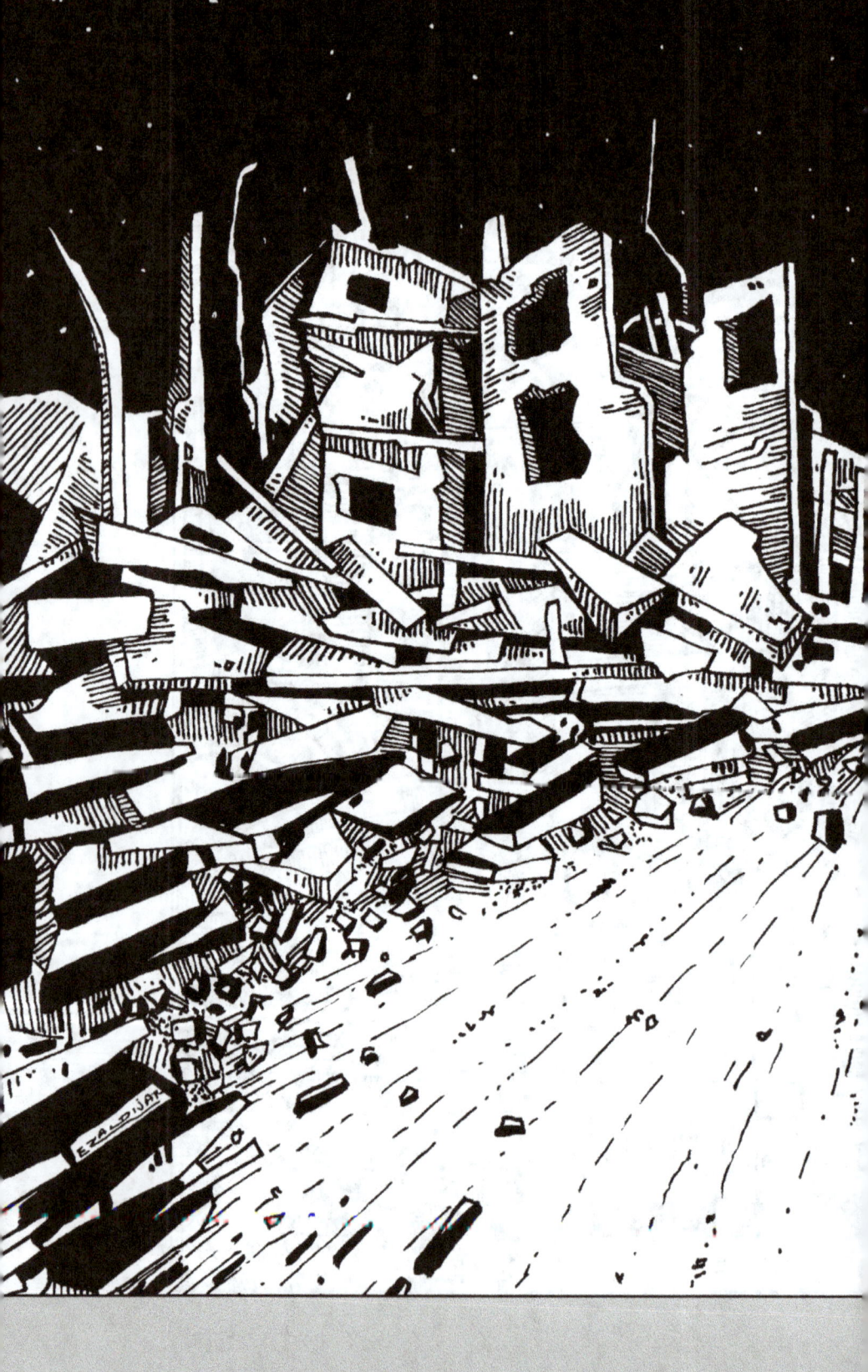

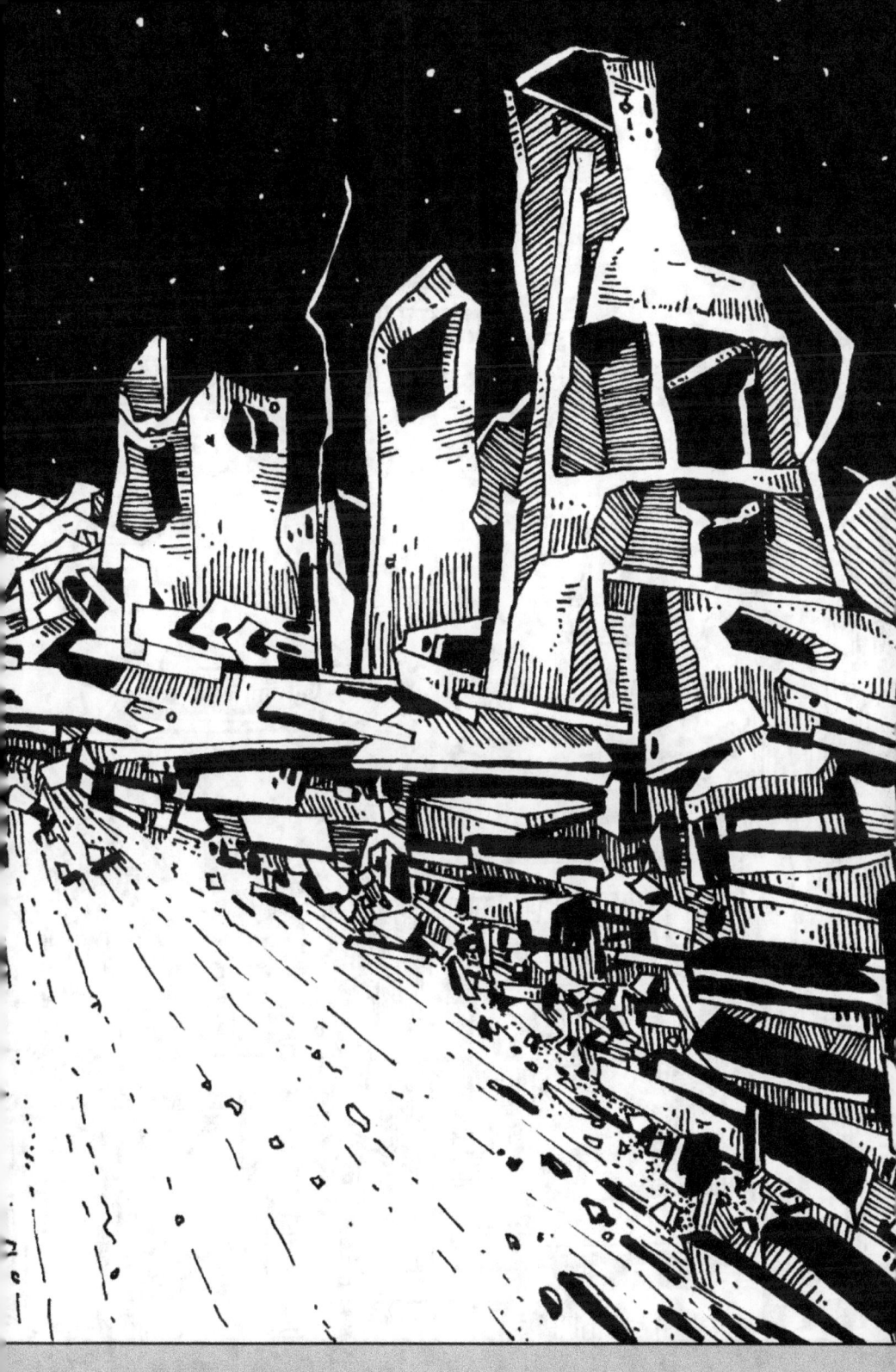

Ruins and decadence

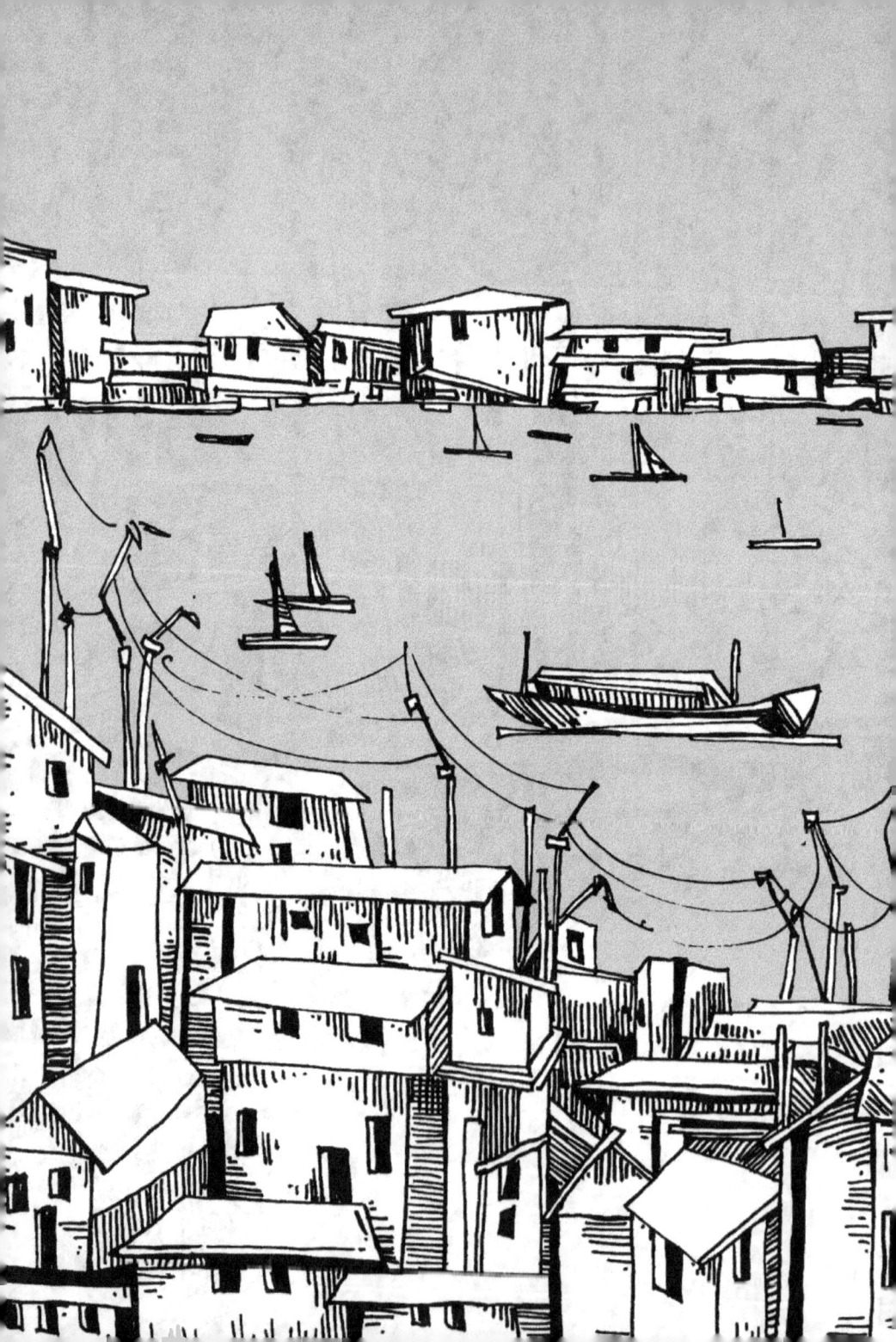

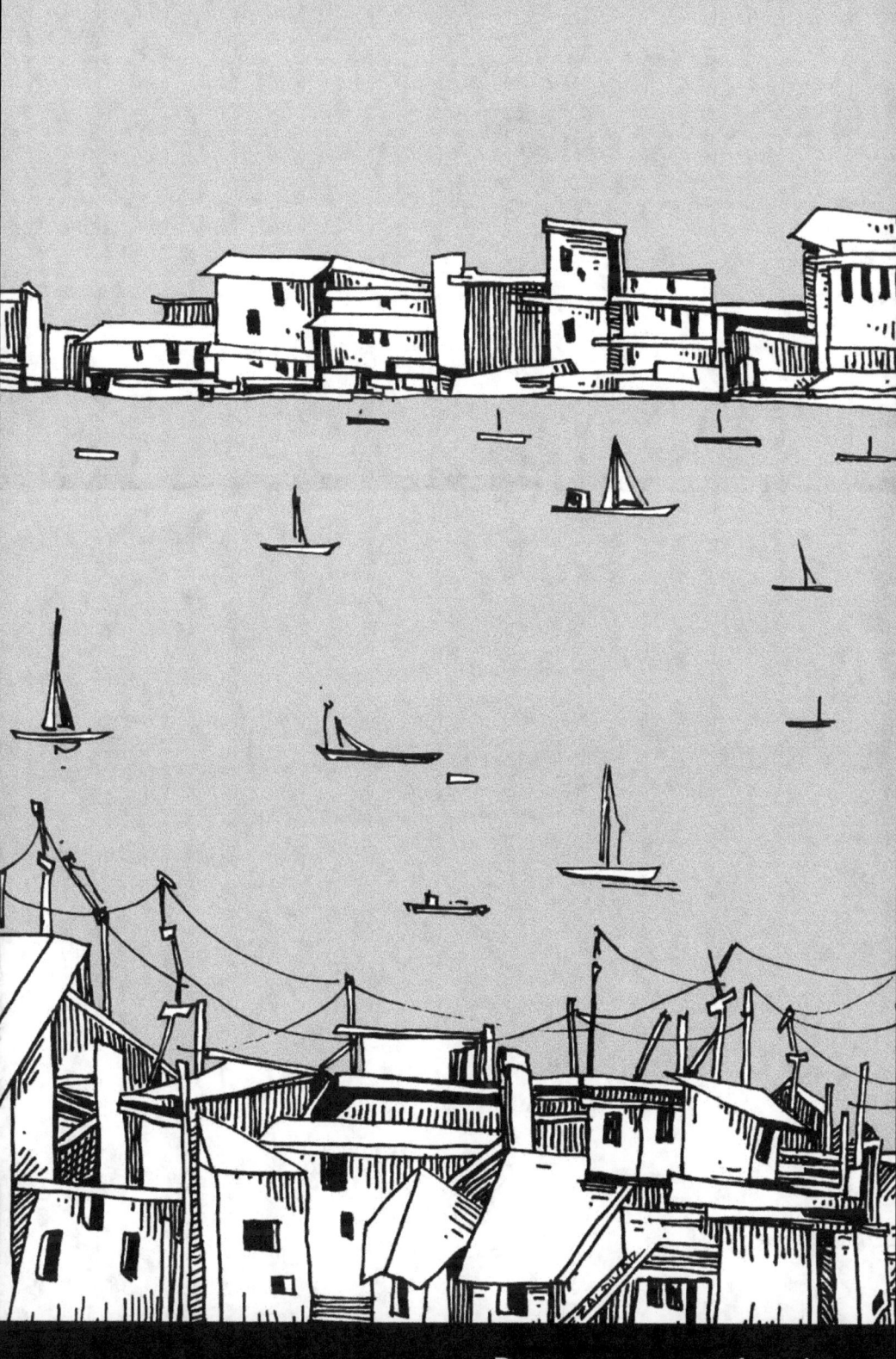

Between two banks

— It is not the end —

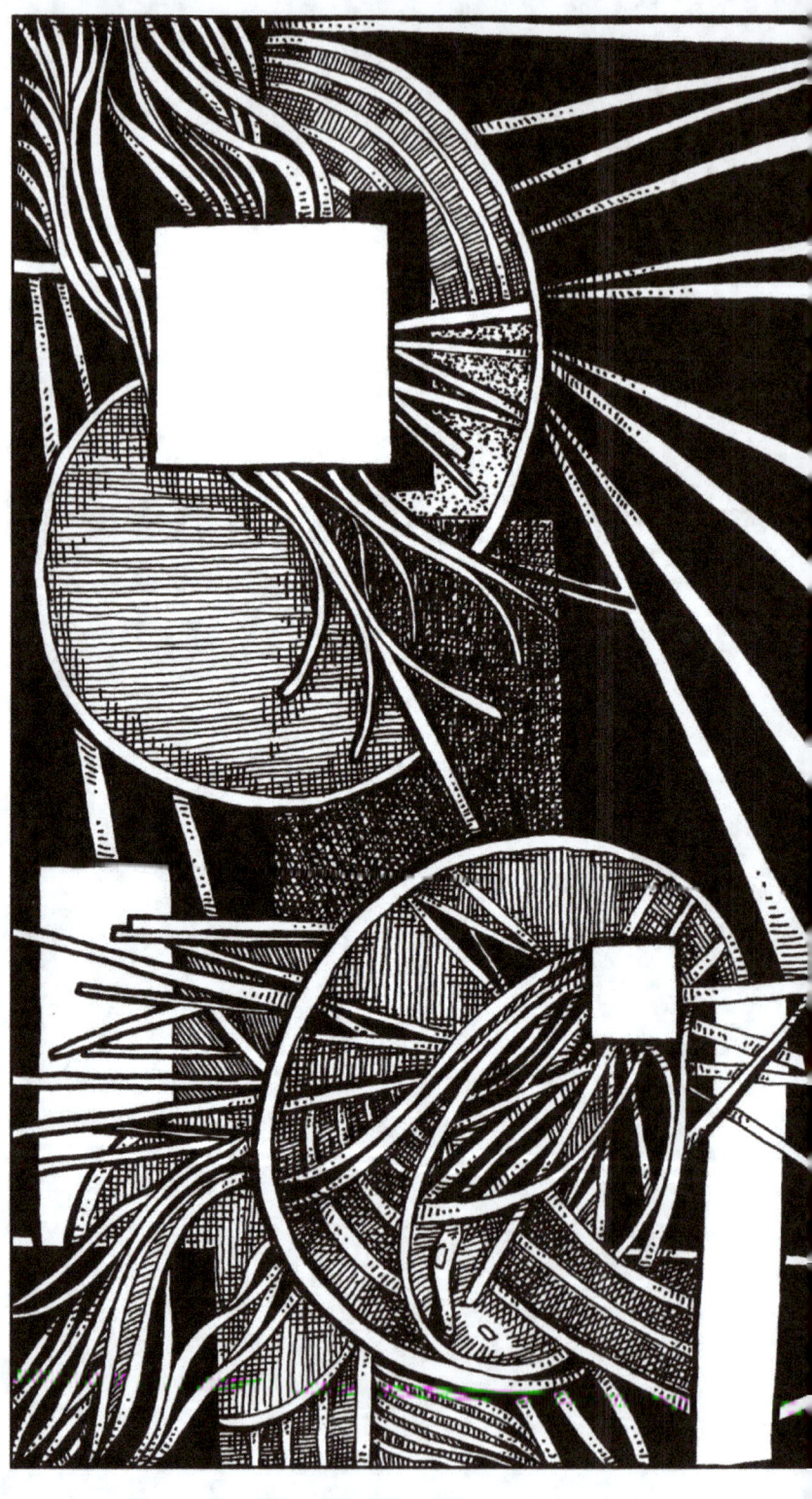

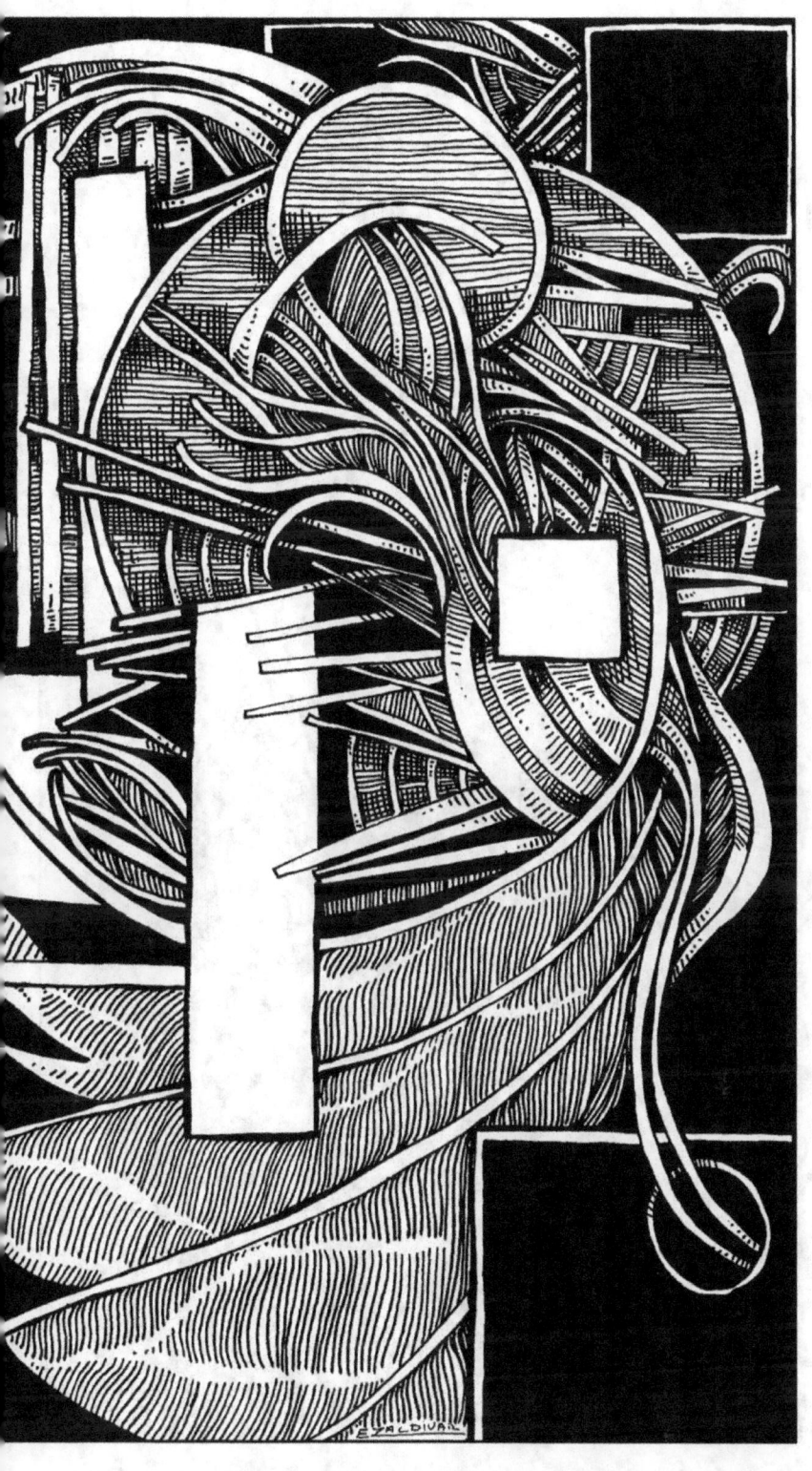

A line is an unfinished journey in the universe

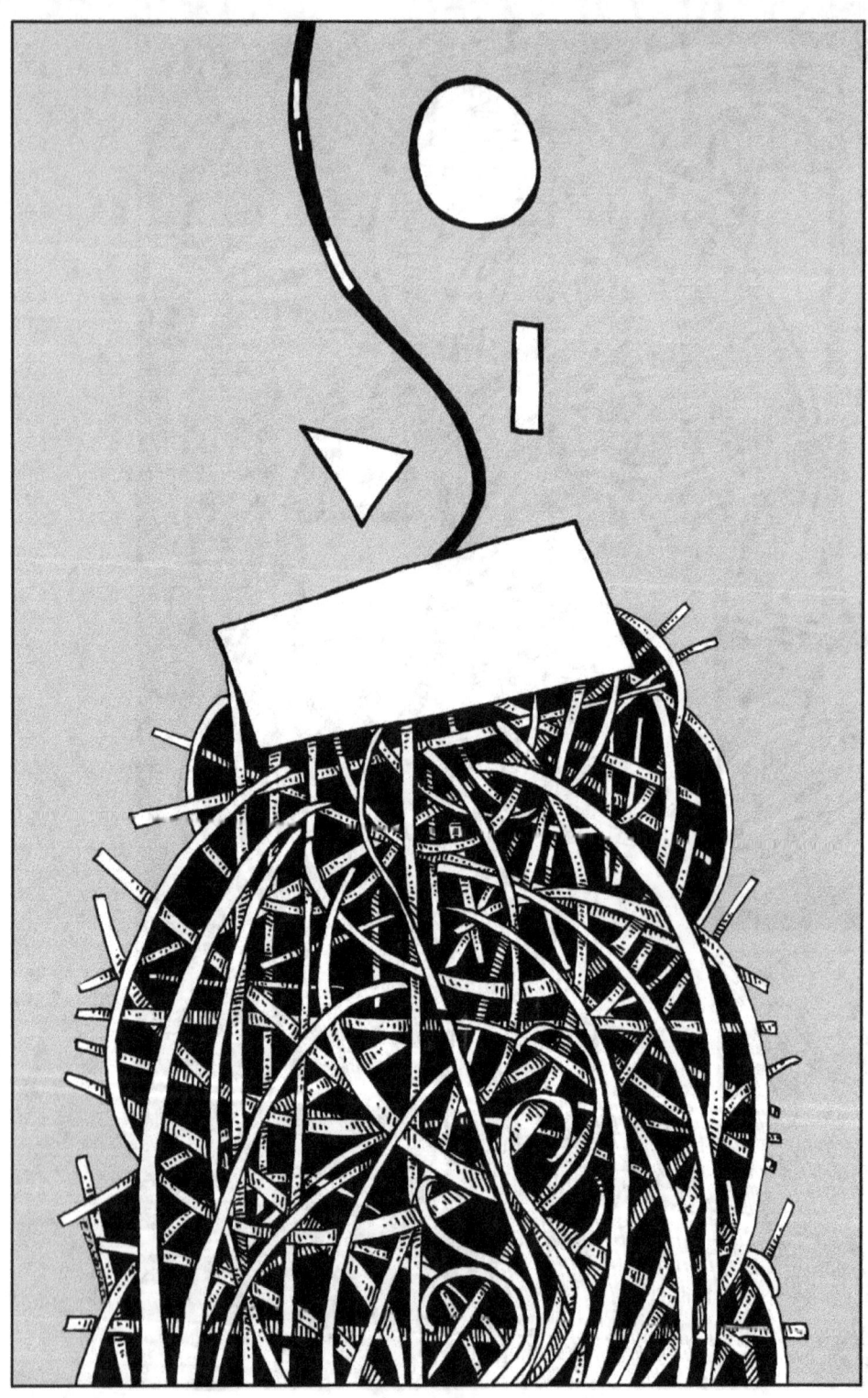

Balance

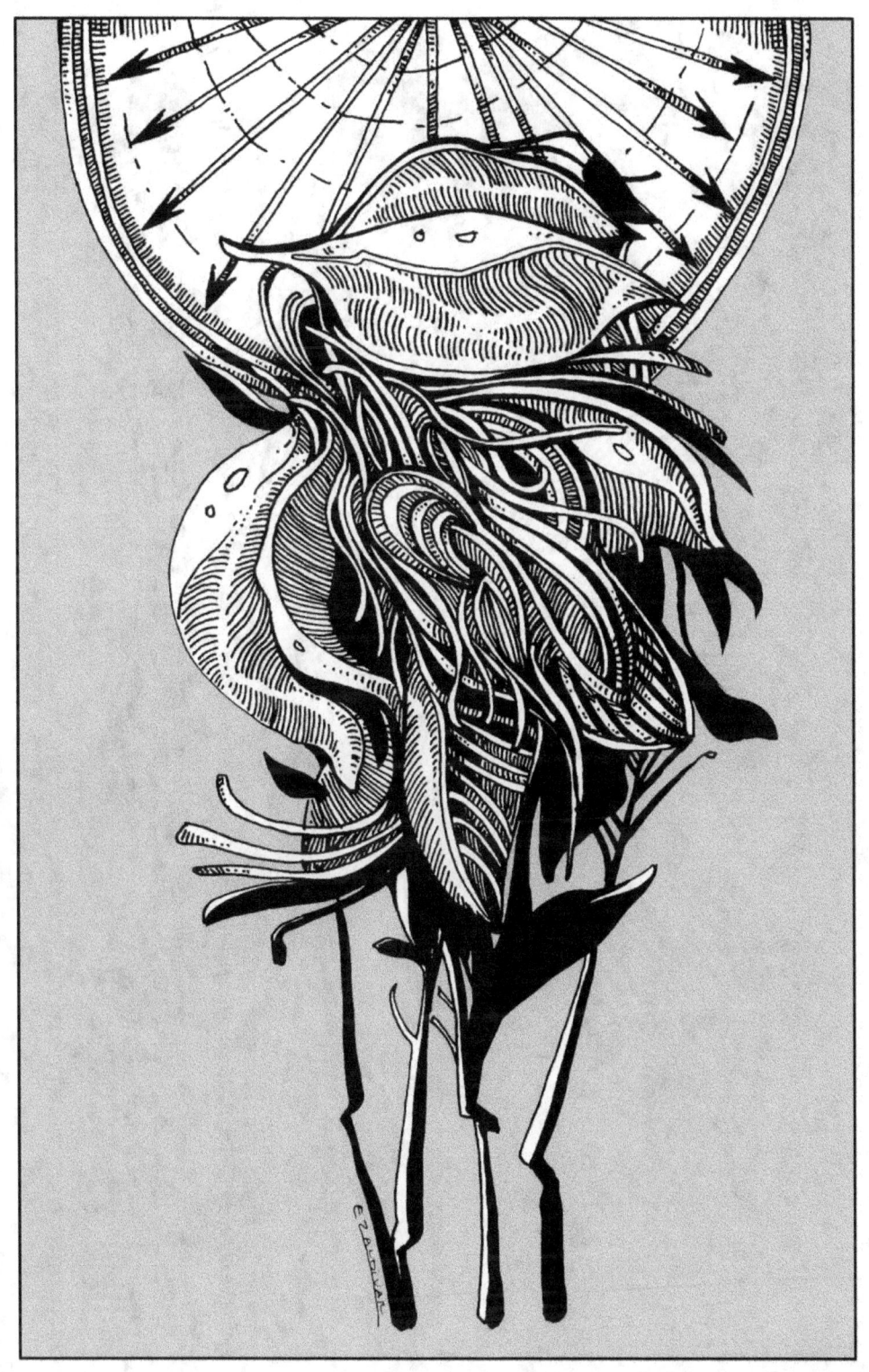

About time

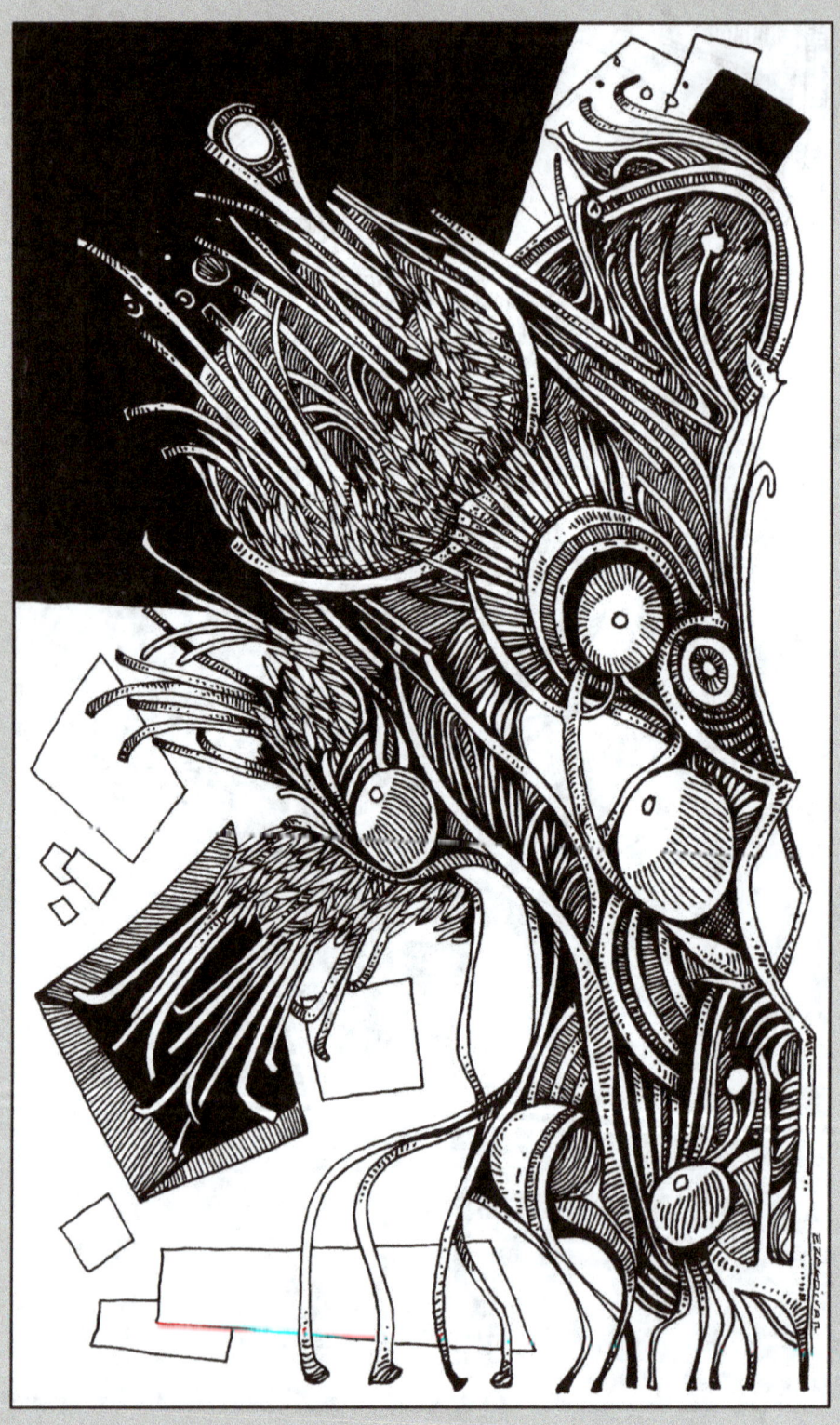

Intuition and metaphysics

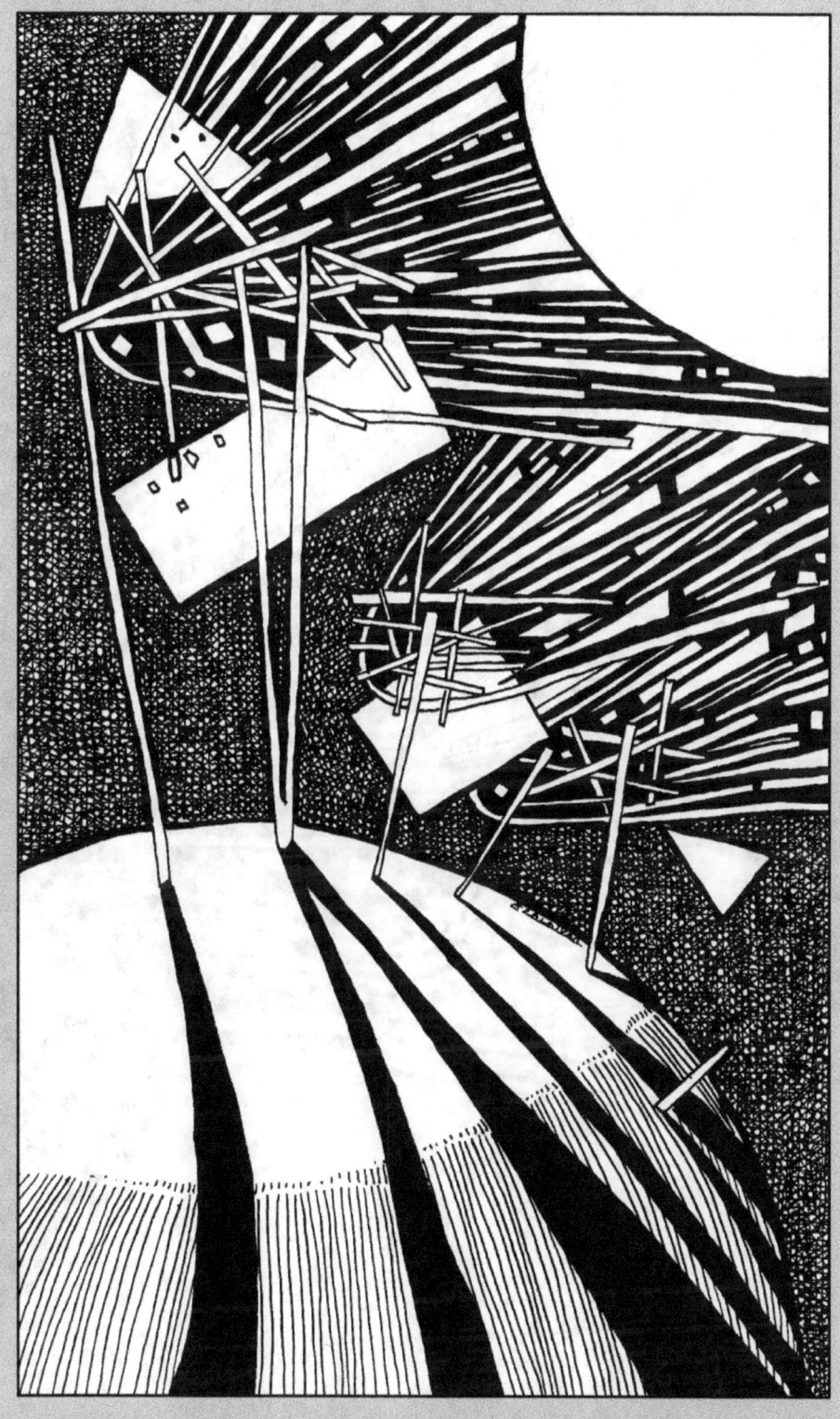

Vacuum energy

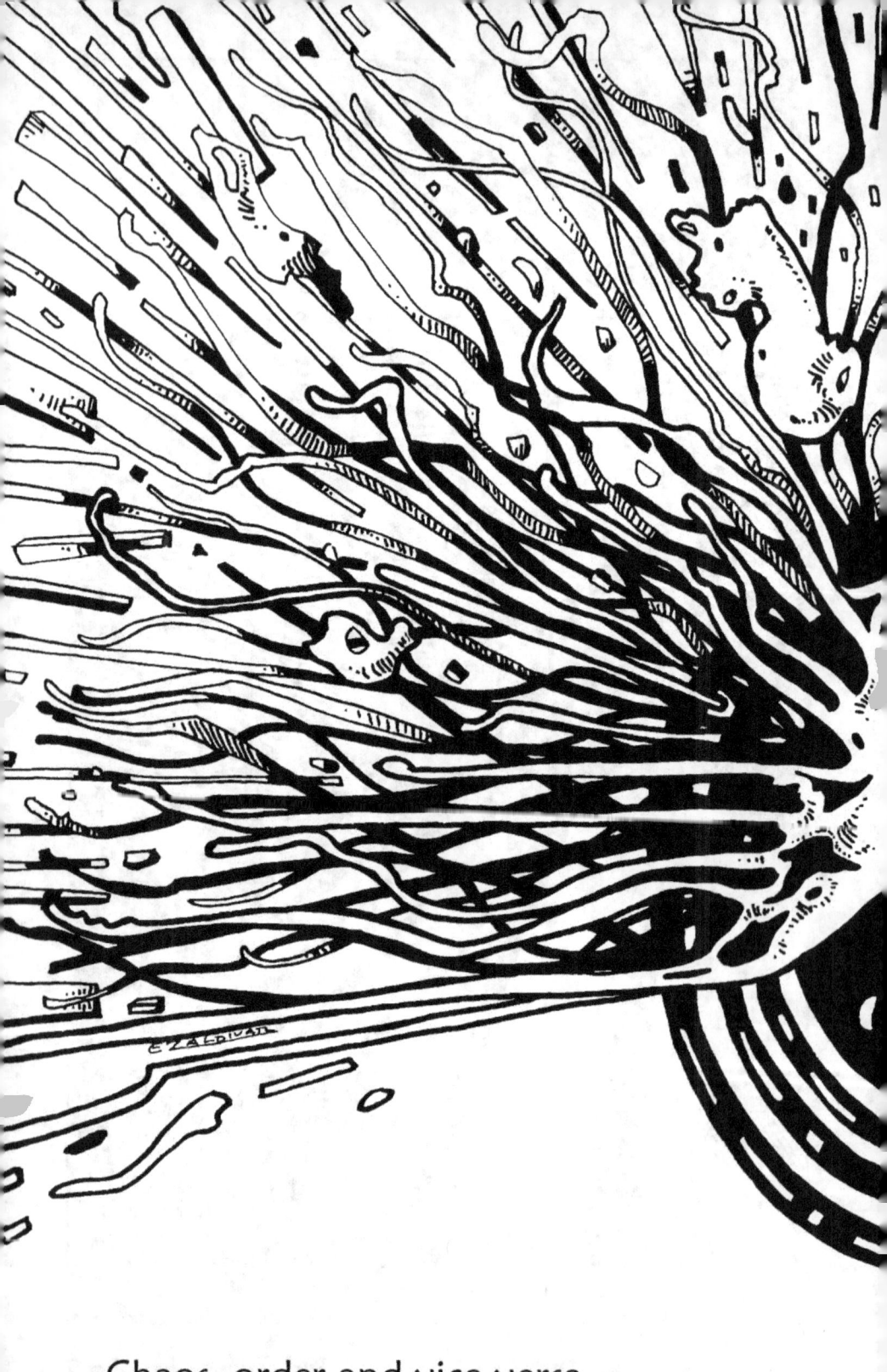

Chaos, order and vice versa

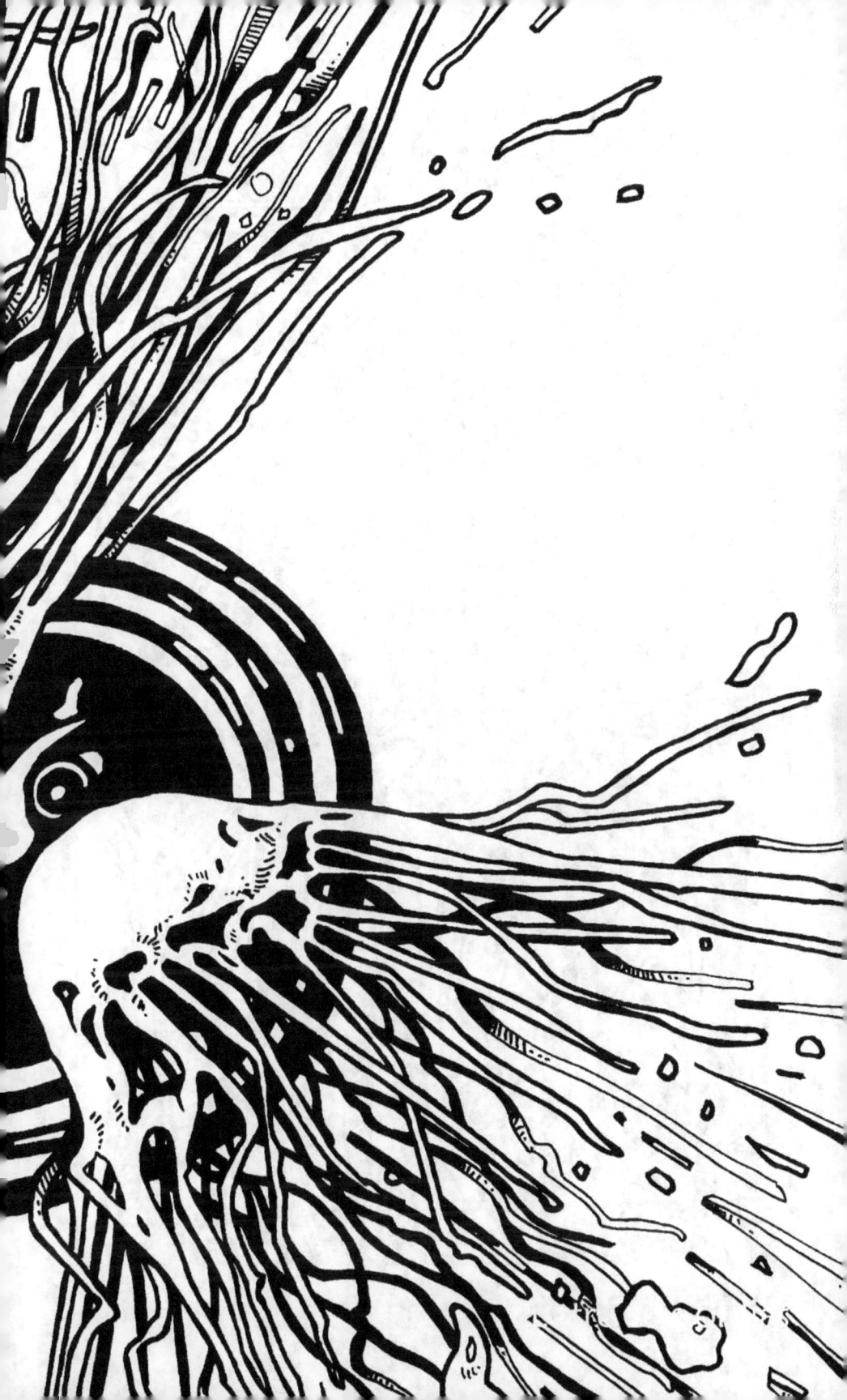

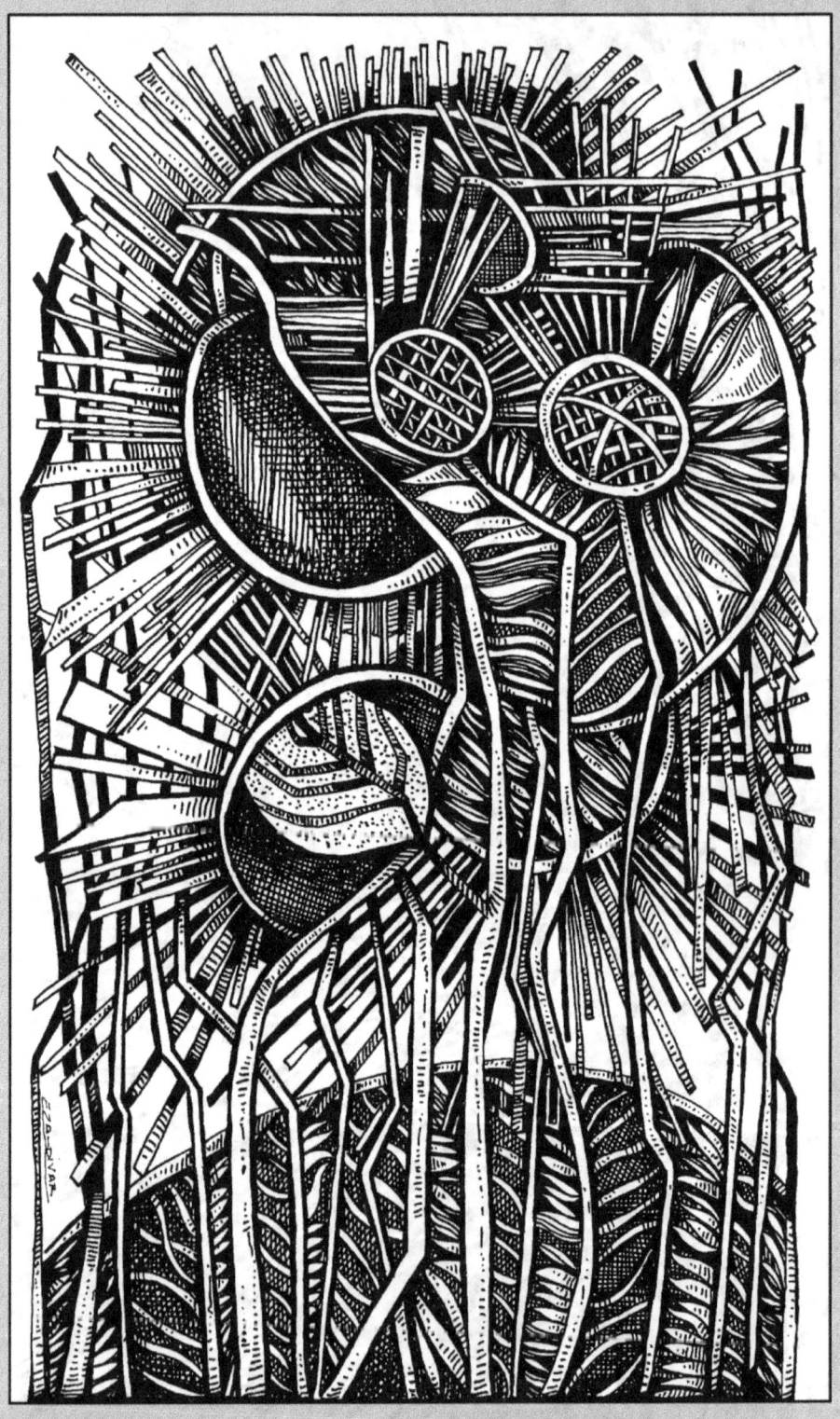

Nature in deconstruction

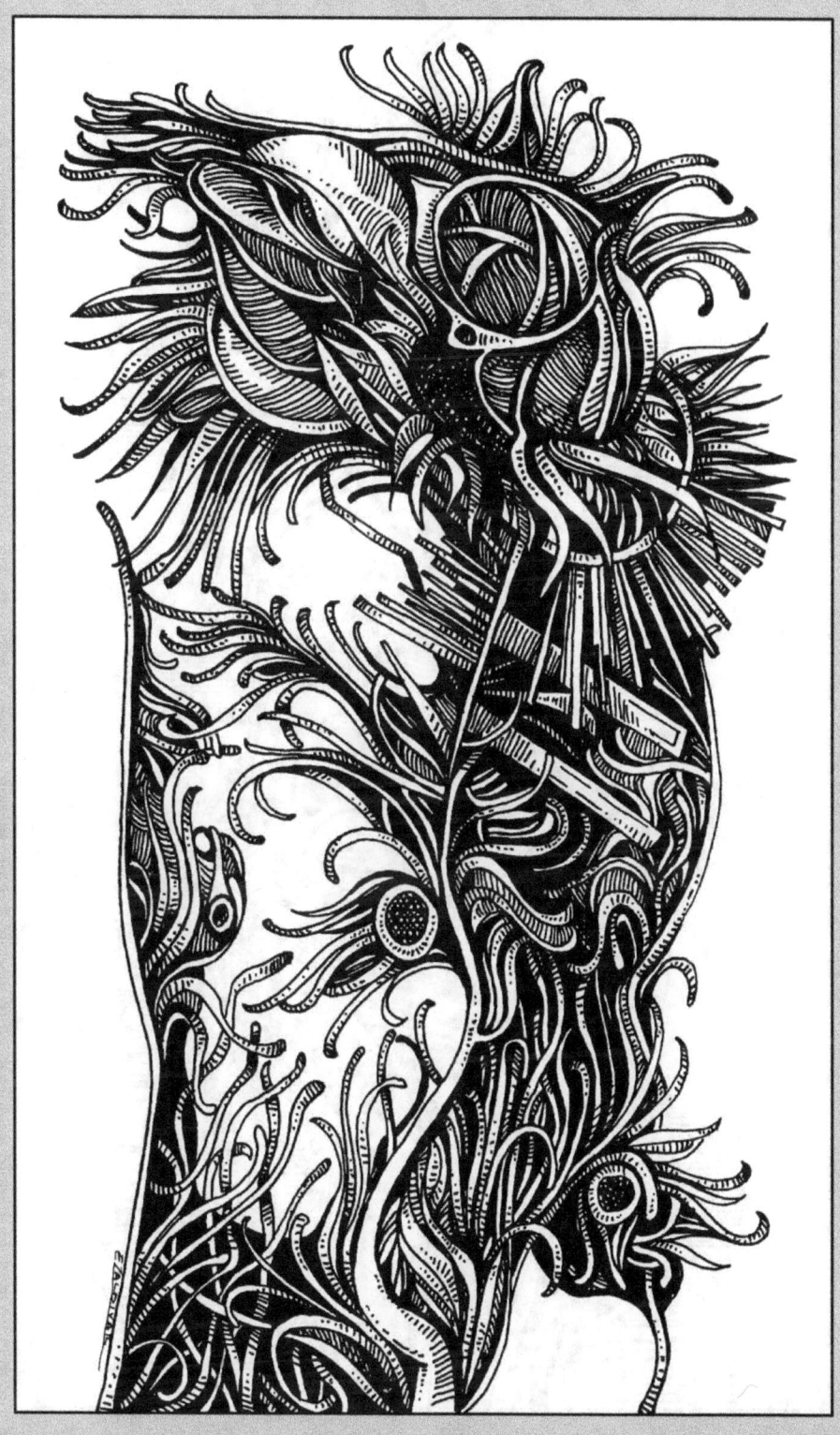

Mutations

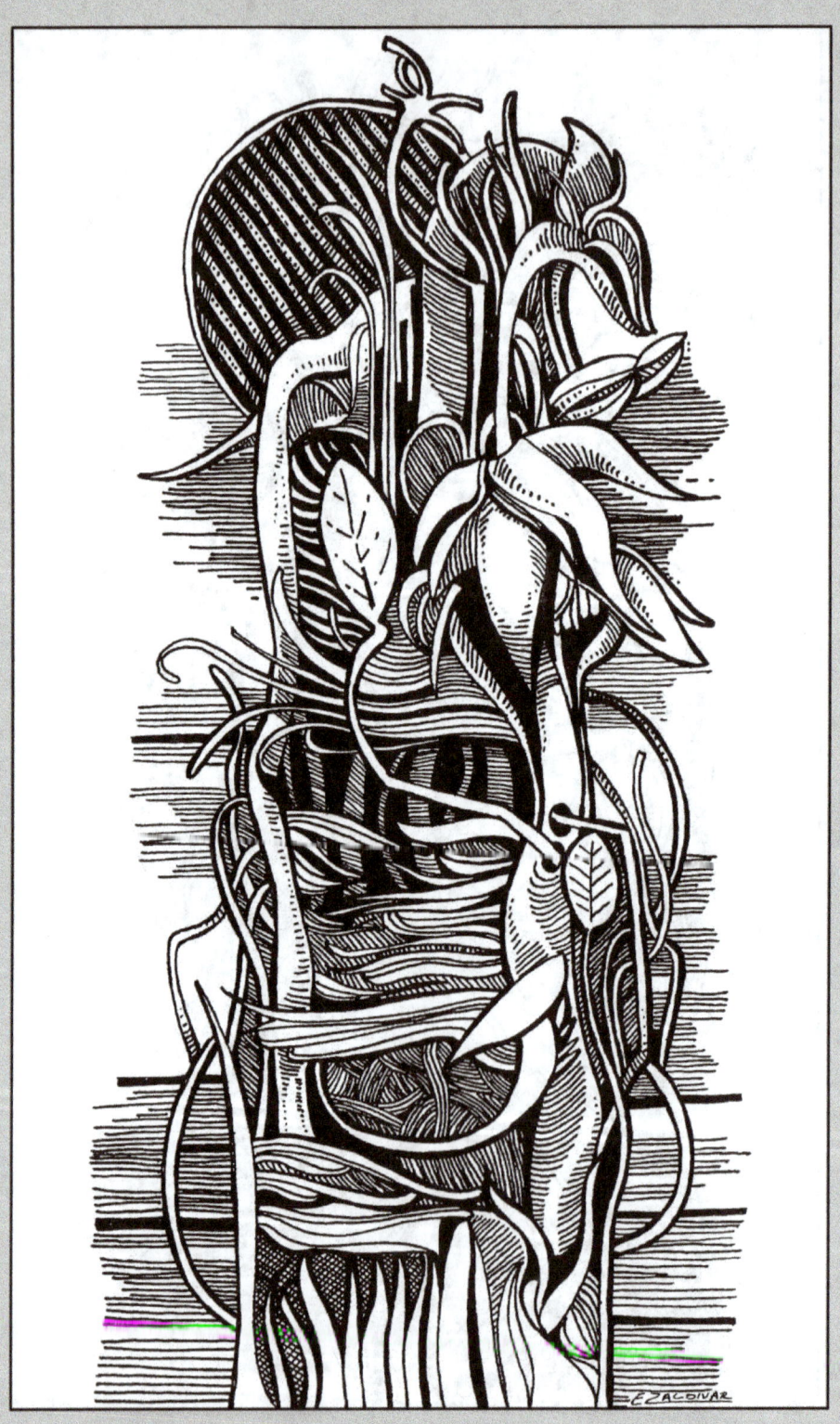

Amorphous plant

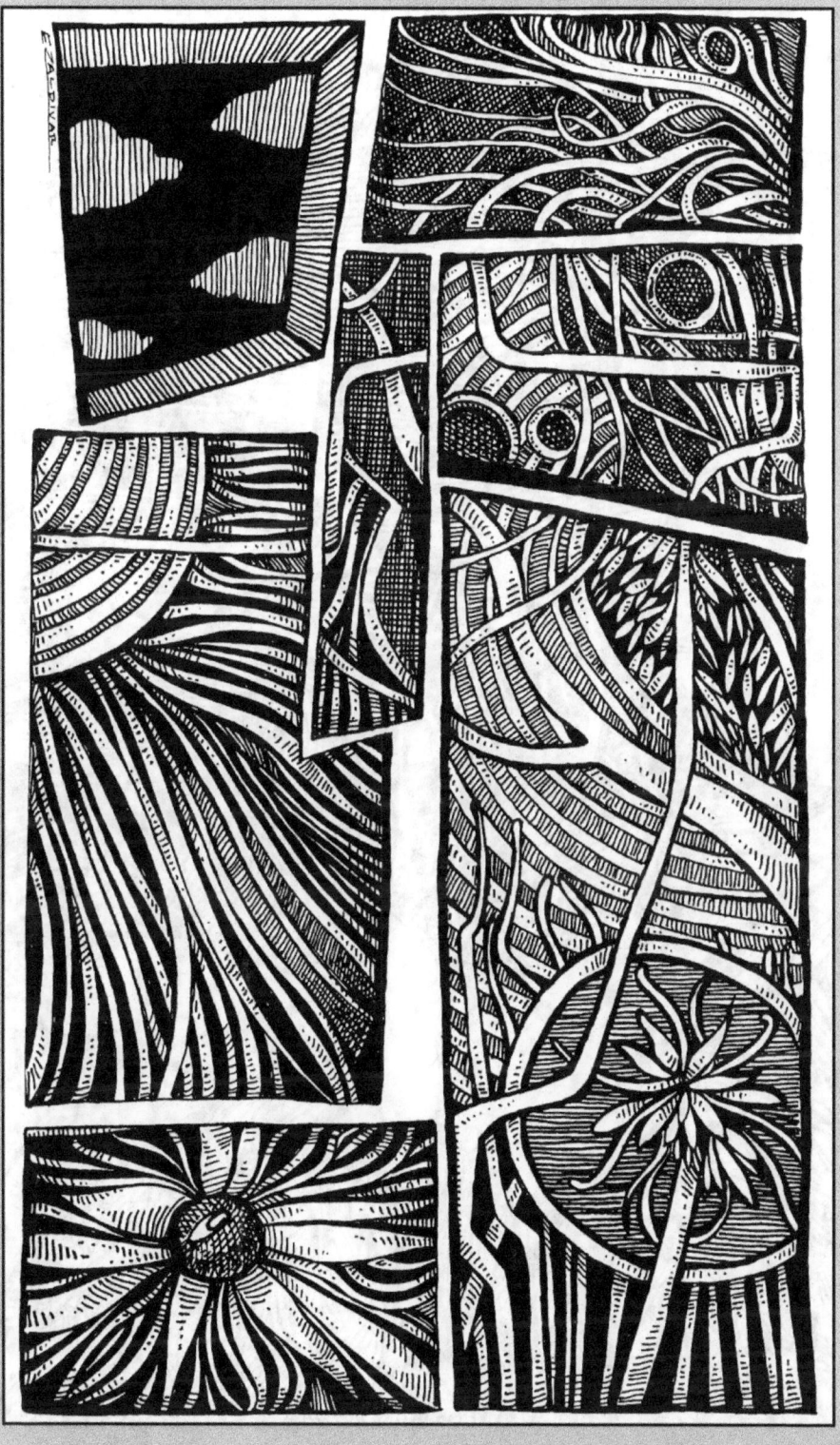

Daedalus

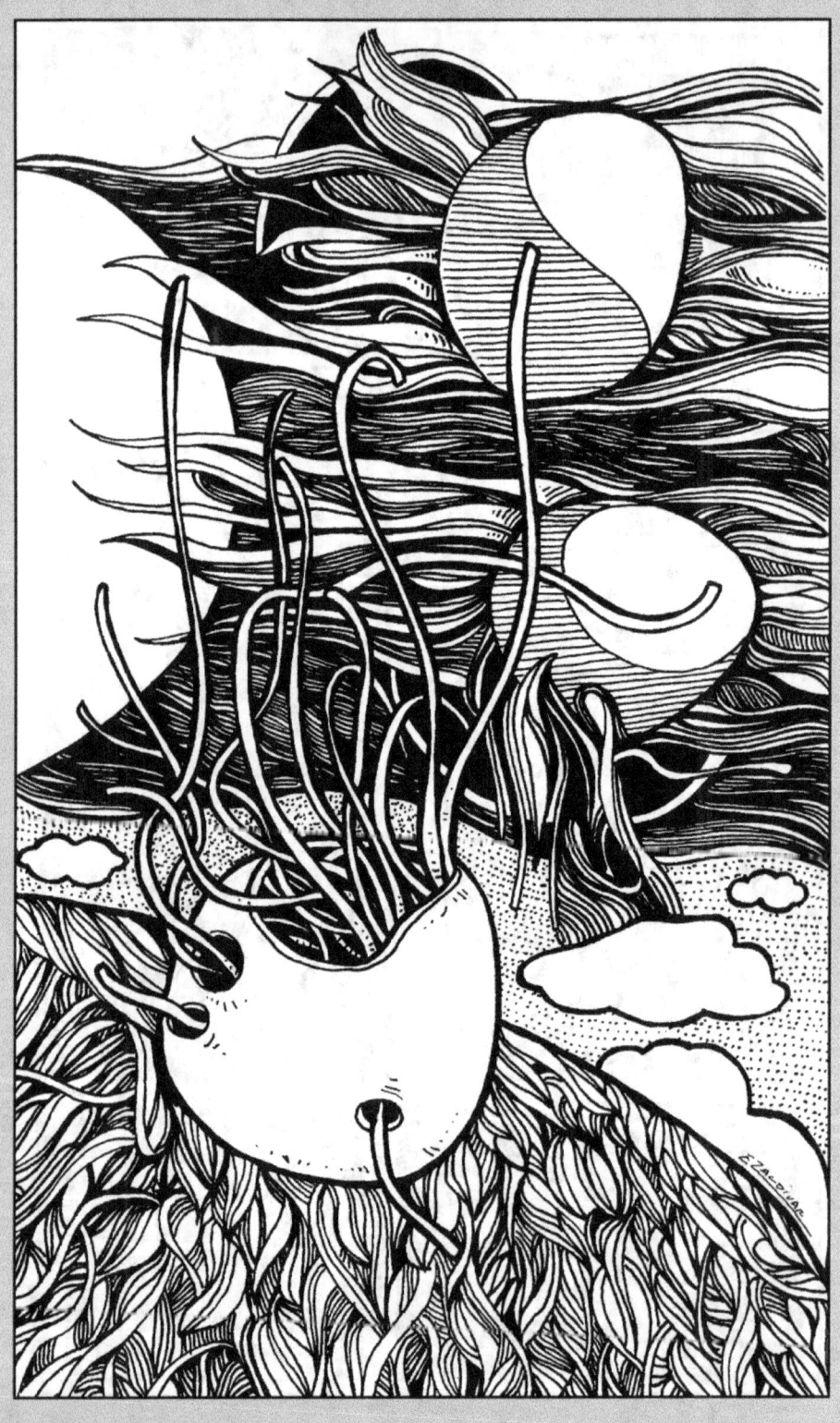

Universe in movement

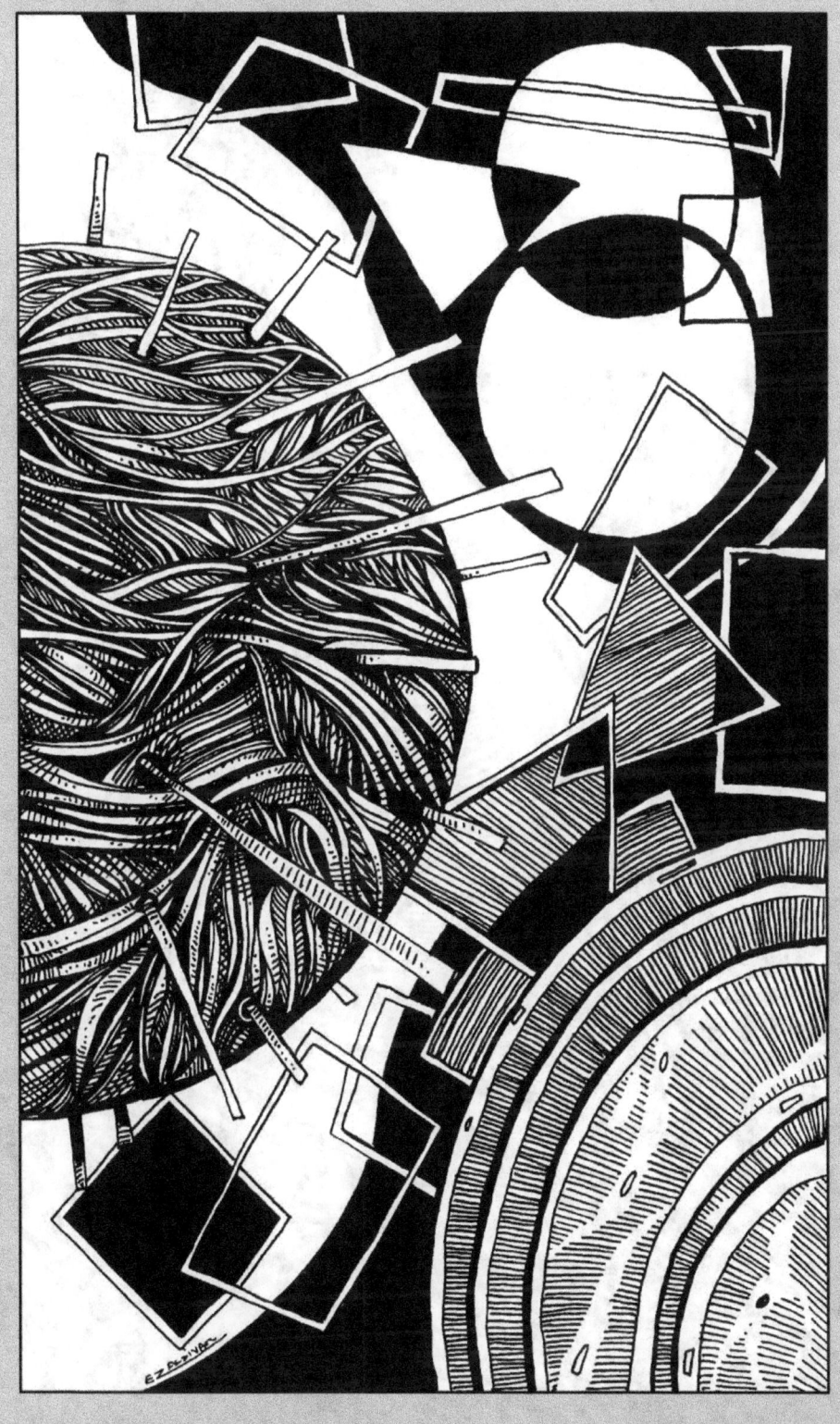

Weightlessness

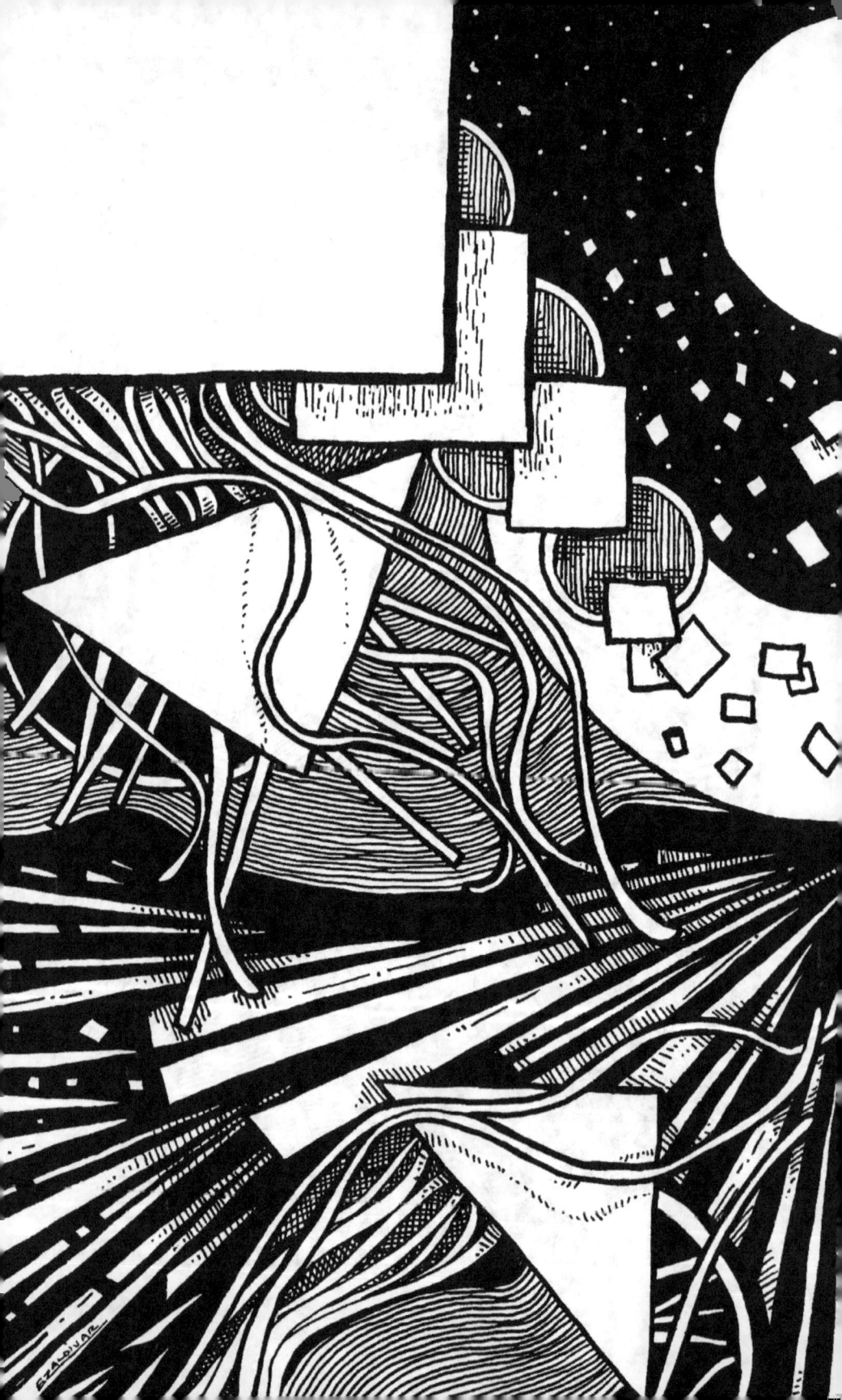

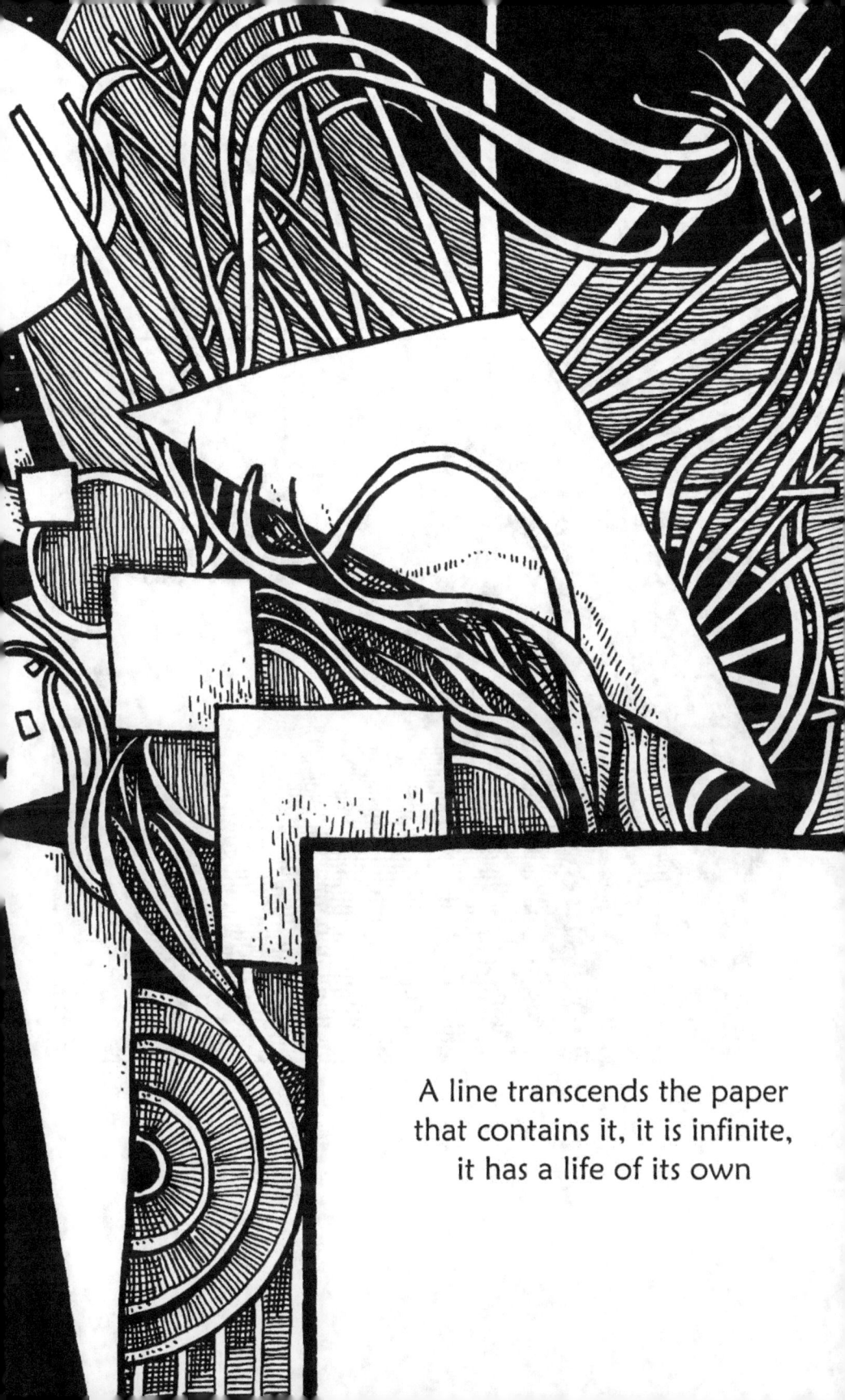

A line transcends the paper
that contains it, it is infinite,
it has a life of its own

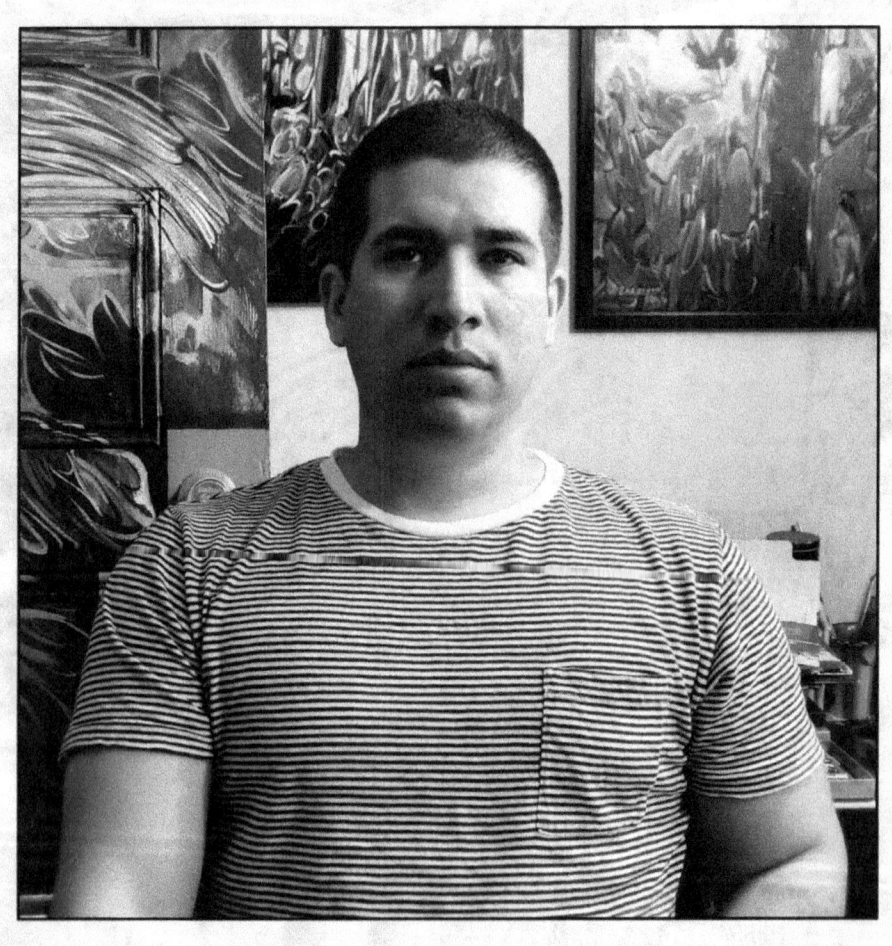

Enrique Zaldivar is a Cuban painter and draftsman. A graduate of The Professional Academy of Fine Arts El Alba in Holquin, he currently lives in the United States.

To date, he has had several exhibitions, both individually and in groups. His works appear in private collections, institutions, and corporations within the USA, and throughout the world. They have transcended the borders of his present home into Canada and Mexico, and also reside in Argentina, The Dominican Republic, France, Italy, Peru and Spain.

Enrique's art is characterized by a uniquely inquisitive look at the world that surrounds him, as well as a drive to recreate and show its wide range of situations.

In each work, he reveals his philosophy of life and his vision of things, seeking to deepen the universe inherent to each person... Not from a distance, but from the personal and introspective.

Although the visual representations of human beings are almost totally absent from his work -- He reflects it as implicit in nature, and as an inseparable part of what is universal.

The paintings and drawings of Zaldivar embody a poetic and philosophical charge that encourages interpretation and dialogue.

To learn more visit: www.enriquezaldivar.com

www.ingramcontent.com/pod-product-compliance
Lightning Source LLC
Chambersburg PA
CBHW071322220526
45468CB00001B/469